Your iPod Life

A guide to the best iPod accessories from Playlist

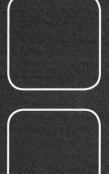

Dan Frakes

Peachpit
Press

Your iPod Life
A guide to the best iPod accessories from Playlist

Dan Frakes

Published in association with Playlist
http://playlistmag.com/

Peachpit Press
1249 Eighth Street
Berkeley, CA 94710
510/524-2178
800/283-9444
510/524-2221 (fax)

Find us on the World Wide Web at: www.peachpit.com
To report errors, please send a note to errata@peachpit.com

Peachpit Press is a division of Pearson Education

Project editor: Clifford Colby
Production editor: Myrna Vladic
Compositor: Maureen Forys, Happenstance Type-O-Rama
Copy editor: Elissa Rabellino
Cover design: Charlene Charles-Will
Interior design: Kim Scott with Maureen Forys
Photo editor: Andrei Pasternak

ISBN 0-321-39470-4

9 8 7 6 5 4 3 2 1

Printed and bound in the United States of America

To Amanda C, Bill C, Chris B, Curt P, Janet R (and her team), Jason S, Jim D, Jon S, Kasey G, Mat H, Peter C, Phil M, Rick L, and Sean G, for making Playlist go. (If I forgot anyone, my apologies.)

To my wife, Jennifer, for putting up with my crazy schedule while I worked on this book.

Contents

About Playlist

Playlist (playlistmag.com) is a Web site from the editors of *Macworld* magazine that's devoted entirely to the iPod and iTunes, for both Mac and Windows users. The site covers the latest in iPod-related news; features a timely iPod blog written by noted iPod expert Christopher Breen; provides a healthy supply of tips, tricks, and how-to articles; and offers a massive collection of hands-on reviews of new iPod accessories.

When it comes to rating products, we don't evaluate them based on press photography or snazzy press releases; we use each and every product, and our reviewers tap their comprehensive knowledge of the various iPod-related product categories to point out which products are worth your money and which simply aren't.

Heading up Playlist's reviews department is Dan Frakes, this book's author. He's built up a remarkable expertise in finding the best iPod gadgets out there and has applied it to choosing products for this book.

Playlist Review URLs

Each product entry in this book includes a URL to the respective vendor's Web site. But Playlist has more to say about many of these products than fits here. At the back of the book, you'll find a page named "Playlist Review URLs" that lists each product along with a four-digit product number. By typing that number after the Playlist URL—in the form *playlistmag.com/####*—in your Web browser, you'll automatically be taken to Playlist's online resource page for that product. From there you'll be able to see our full review, and for many products, you'll even see shopping links to help you find the lowest price.

And if there's an accessory you *didn't* find in this book—including products that might have arrived after the book went to press—be sure to visit playlistmag.com, where you'll find ongoing coverage of the best (and worst) that the iPod market has to offer.

—Jason Snell
Editorial Director, Playlist

Introduction

If you had told me back in 2001, when the iPod was first introduced, that someday I'd be writing a book about *accessories* for the player, I would have gotten a good laugh out of the suggestion. And yet here we are, well over 30 million iPods later, with that book in your hands.

Fact is, when you purchase an iPod, you're not just buying a killer portable music player. You're also gaining access to the most diverse and plentiful array of aftermarket accessories for any product I can remember. Cases, speakers, headphones, chargers, cables, adapters—if you can think of it…well, someone else probably already did and is selling it right now. In fact, according to Apple, there are now more than 1000 accessories for the iPod on the market. You read that right: *more than 1000 accessories*. This is a billion-dollar market dedicated to addressing (and, let's be honest, *creating*) your every iPod-related desire.

With so many options, how do you figure out which of these products are worth your hard-earned cash? At Playlist (www.playlistmag.com), we review iPod and digital music products every day, figuring out which ones work and which ones don't; which are worth the money and which aren't; which stand out from the crowd and which are just more of the same. We give our readers the lowdown on products so that they can spend less time wondering which ones to buy and more time enjoying their music. *Your iPod Life* is our overview of some of the best iPod-related products we've seen—the cream of the accessory crop, so to speak—in handy book form. If something is included here, that means we've tried it and feel it's worth singling out. Put simply, *Your iPod Life* is our way of helping you to spend your iPod budget on the best stuff.

We've divided this book into chapters based on product type to make it easier for you to find what you want:

- "Cases": Ways to carry your iPod and keep it safe

- "Portable Speakers": Ways to listen to your iPod out loud, on the go

- "Home Speakers": Speakers that don't fit in your suitcase—iPod-specific systems as well as traditional "computer" speakers

- "Headphones": High-quality upgrades for your iPod's earbuds

- "Auto Accessories": Cool toys for listening to your iPod in your car

- "General Accessories": All the other gizmos and gadgets that let you do more with your iPod

For each product, we tell you what it is, why we like it, how much it costs, which iPod(s) it works with, and a URL for finding out more about it.

Before you start flipping through the product pages, take a look at the "iPod Models" section (which follows this introduction). Once you've located *your* iPod, note its "Compatibility Icon." This icon shows you which of the products in this book will work with your iPod.

One more thing: With the iPod market showing no signs of slowing down, new stuff is released on literally a daily basis. We can't send you a new book each week, but we *can* direct you to PlaylistMag.com for the latest in product reviews and iPod news. I'm not just talking about accessories, either—new iPods themselves are released at a surprising rate. For example, in the few weeks before we went to press, Apple released two new models, the iPod nano and the latest full-size iPod, which supports video. The product information included in *Your iPod Life* reflects compatibility and availability at the time we went to print, but vendors are releasing new products, and newly compatible versions of existing products, every day. Visit playlistmag.com for everything that's happened since we had to put down our pens and stop working.

Thanks for reading. If you have comments or questions, e-mail us at YouriPodLife@playlistmag.com.

—Dan Frakes
Senior Reviews Editor, Playlist

iPod Models

To make it easier for you to determine if a particular product included in this book will work with *your* iPod, each product entry provides icons indicating which iPods are compatible. Here is a brief overview of each iPod model along with its Compatibility Icon. (If, after browsing this section, you're still not sure which iPod model you have, Apple has a Knowledge Base article at http://docs. info.apple.com/article.html?artnum=61688 that can help you figure it out.)

Note that Compatibility Icons indicate specific iPod *models;* however, each model may come in different physical *sizes*. For example, the iPod with color display was available in 20 GB and 60 GB versions; the latter is thicker than the former. You'll need to check with the vendor of an accessory or the product's packaging to make sure you get the one that fits your iPod.

Current iPod Models

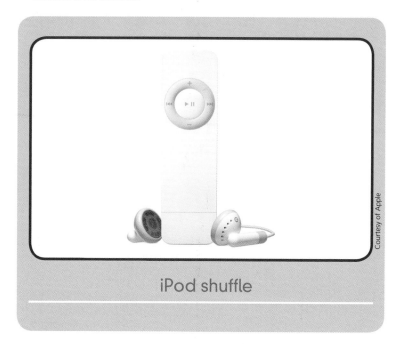

Courtesy of Apple

iPod shuffle

The least expensive and smallest (in both physical size and storage capacity) iPod ever, the shuffle uses flash memory instead of a hard-disk drive, so it has no moving parts. It also has no screen, uses tactile buttons rather than the famous Click Wheel of larger iPods, and has a standard USB plug rather than Apple's versatile dock connector. But despite these omissions, it's still very much an iPod: It sounds great, it syncs with iTunes, and you can even store data files on it. Because it's small, durable, and relatively inexpensive, the iPod shuffle is a favorite for the gym (it's lightweight and never skips), for kids (they won't break it), and as a second iPod (just in case you lose it). (Battery life: 12 hours.)

Versions: 512 MB (approx. 120 songs), $99; 1 GB (approx. 240 songs), $129.

iPod nano

Courtesy of Apple

The nano, released in late 2005 as a replacement for the best-selling iPod mini, is quite possibly the most stunning iPod yet, thanks to a design that combines many of the features of full-size iPods with the best of the iPod shuffle. Like the shuffle, the nano uses flash memory, so it doesn't skip and can take a few bumps and bruises. But like the larger iPods, the nano includes a crisp color screen—albeit a significantly smaller version—that displays album art, your favorite photos, and the iPod's famous interface; it also includes Apple's Click Wheel controller and dock connector port. All of this in a tiny package the size of a business card and just over a quarter of an inch thick. With its small size and sleek black or white front (and, of course, chrome back), the nano is just as stylish as it is functional. If you don't need the huge capacity or photo/video features of a full-size iPod, the nano is tough to resist. (Battery life: music, 14 hours; onscreen photo slide shows, 4 hours.)

Versions: 2 GB (approx. 500 songs), $199; 4 GB (approx. 1,000 songs), $249.

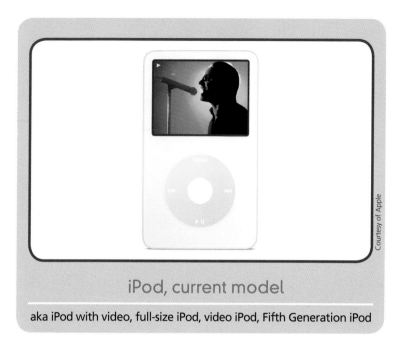

Courtesy of Apple

iPod, current model

aka iPod with video, full-size iPod, video iPod, Fifth Generation iPod

This multimedia powerhouse takes all the features that made previous iPods great—LCD display, Click Wheel, dock connector, huge storage capacity, great sound quality, and more recently, photo storage and viewing—and adds the ability to play back video on its bigger and brighter screen. Apple accomplished all of this while also making the newest iPod even thinner than the previous model—it actually looks like a super-sized version of the iPod nano (and it's available in the same white or black finish). And with the right accessories, you can record audio and even view your iPod-hosted photos and videos on a TV screen or projector. Because the full-size iPod uses a hard-disk drive, it's not as ideal for exercise or other active uses as its smaller siblings, but it's the iPod to get if you need massive storage capacity or A/V functionality. (Battery life, 60 GB: music, 20 hours; onscreen photo slide shows, 4 hours; onscreen video playback, 3 hours. Battery life, 30 GB: music, 14 hours; onscreen photo slide shows, 3 hours; onscreen video playback, 2 hours.)

Versions: 30 GB (approx. 7,000 songs), $299; 60 GB (approx. 15,000 songs), $399.

Previous iPod Models

iPod (scroll wheel) and iPod (touch wheel)

aka First Generation and Second Generation, respectively

The original iPod (2001) and its immediate successor (2002) were similar in that they each had a round scroll wheel surrounded by four physical buttons (Menu, Forward, Play/Pause, Back). The major difference was that on the original iPod, that scroll wheel was mechanical—it actually rotated. On Second Generation models, it was a stationary, touch-sensitive wheel (hence the iPod's official name). Both models connected to a computer via a standard FireWire cable; the Second Generation model included a protective plastic cover for the FireWire port.

Versions: First Generation, 5 GB and 10 GB; Second Generation, 10 GB and 20 GB.

iPod (dock connector)

aka Third Generation, Horizontal Buttons

The third generation of iPods (2003) featured a significant redesign. The most obvious change was the shift from a scroll wheel surrounded by physical buttons to four touch-sensitive, backlit buttons arranged in a horizontal row *above* the scroll wheel. These iPods were also the first to include Apple's versatile dock connector port on the bottom (consequently eliminating the FireWire port), as well as a new remote/headphone jack that would be found on all subsequent full-size and mini iPods until the recent nano and video-capable models did away with it.

Versions: 10 GB, 15 GB, 20 GB, 30 GB, 40 GB.

iPod mini

The iPod mini was a significant departure from the minimalist design of previous iPods: Instead of a sleek white face and chrome back, the two iPod mini generations featured a brushed-aluminum body available in either five (2004) or four (2005) colors. The mini was also the first iPod to sacrifice storage capacity for smaller size and the first to feature the now-famous Click Wheel: a touch-sensitive scroll wheel with the iPod's Play/Pause, Forward, Back, and Menu buttons embedded in it. However, the mini inherited its larger sibling's dock connector port and headphone/remote jack, making it compatible with many existing accessories. Because of its sleek shape, small size, stylish colors, and lower price compared with those of full-size models, the iPod mini quickly became the best selling iPod and remained so until Apple replaced it with the nano in late 2005.

Versions: original 4 GB in silver, gold, pink, blue, green; later 4 GB and 6 GB in silver and brighter versions of pink, blue, green.

iPod (Click Wheel)

aka Fourth Generation

The fourth generation of iPods (2005) was the second major redesign of the full-size iPod line. Gone were the white scroll wheel and four horizontal buttons of Third Generation models, replaced by a larger version of the iPod mini's Click Wheel. This was also the first full-size iPod that could be charged and synced via USB.

Versions: 20 GB, 40 GB; Special Edition U2, 20 GB.

iPod photo *and* iPod with color display

Apple released two official photo-capable lines: the original, called the iPod photo (2004), and the second, called the iPod with color display (2005). The latter was simply a merging of the previous Fourth Generation and iPod photo lines into a single "color" line. These models all looked and functioned identically to Fourth Generation iPods, except that they had color screens and featured the ability to store and view photos on the iPod, as well as to "project" photo slide shows on a TV via Apple's AV cable or video-output Dock.

Versions: iPod photo, 30 GB, 40 GB, 60 GB; iPod with color display, 20 GB, 60 GB; Special Edition U2, 20 GB.

iPod Special Edition U2

In 2004 and 2005, Apple sold two limited-edition iPods cobranded with the rock band U2. The first was actually a 20 GB Fourth Generation iPod; the second was a 20 GB iPod with color display. These Special Edition iPods differed from the standard versions in that the U2 models were black with a red Click Wheel and had the signatures of the members of U2 engraved on the back. If you've got a U2 iPod, use the Compatibility Icon for Fourth Generation or "color display" iPods—whichever is appropriate—to determine accessory compatibility.

iPod + HP

For a limited time from 2004 to 2005, Hewlett-Packard sold HP-branded iPods, officially called iPod + HP. Apart from the HP logo on the back and different warranty support, these iPods were identical to Apple's own. If you've got an HP-branded iPod, it's either a shuffle or a mini (in which case, it is obvious which of the above categories it belongs in), or a Fourth Generation or photo model. One of the latter, but you're not sure which? If it has a color screen, it's an iPod photo; if not, it's a Fourth Generation. Use the Compatibility Icon for the Apple iPod equivalent to the model you have.

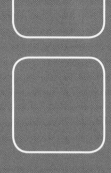

Cases

The iPod is at once a stunning example of stylish product design and an aesthetically delicate object that seems to pick up scratches and smudges from sideways glances. So as much as you may want to show off your iPod, the first accessory most owners buy is a case to keep it safe from harm.

Cases come in many styles, from fine leather flip covers to sporty silicone skins; for many uses, from working out at the gym to carrying in your bag; and for protection against varying degrees of damage, from scratches to smashing. There are even waterproof cases that you can bring along for a dip in the pool. We've chosen some of our favorites of each style, and for each type of iPod, here.

(Note that when an iPod Compatibility Icon is included for a case, it means that a version of the case is *available* for that iPod model; however, the different versions of a case may not be identical to the one pictured. For example, an iPod nano version of a case will likely be much smaller than the full-size version and may have minor aesthetic or functional differences.)

Given the sheer number of cases available for the iPod, we can't even cover all of our favorites here. If you don't find something you like, visit playlistmag.com for reviews of many more.

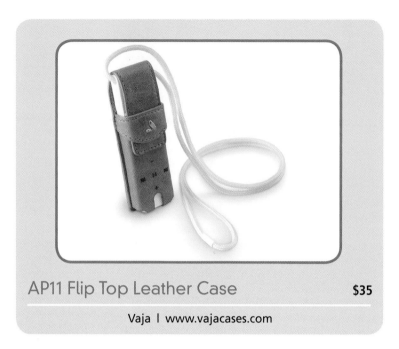

AP11 Flip Top Leather Case $35

Vaja | www.vajacases.com

Vaja's iPod cases are generally more expensive than other cases, but they also tend to be better looking and built well. Vaja's first offering for the iPod shuffle, an Argentinean leather flip case, continues these trends. The AP11 fits your shuffle like a glove, with small icons for the iPod's underlying controls embossed into the leather on the front—you can press the buttons through the case. The flip cover accommodates both the shuffle's standard USB cap and the lanyard cap, so you can carry your AP11-clad shuffle in your pocket or show it off around your neck. And unlike some leather shuffle cases, the AP11 allows you to see the shuffle's indicator light and use the switch on the back. Two versions of the AP11 are available: the textured, shiny Vitelino, available in 15 color choices; and the softer, smoother Analine, with 7 color options. Whichever you choose, Vaja's AP11 is the nicest leather case we've seen for the shuffle.

Apple iPod shuffle Armband
$29

Apple
http://store.apple.com

Apple iPod nano Armband
$29

Apple
http://store.apple.com

A number of companies make "exercise" armbands for the shuffle and nano—the best iPods for exercising since they have no moving parts—but Apple's offerings are typical Apple: simple, attractive, and functional. The shuffle version provides a hard plastic cradle into which you plug your iPod shuffle; a flexible vinyl armband stretches to fit arms 7 to 14 inches around. The nano version holds your nano in a vinyl sleeve that leaves the screen exposed but protects the Click Wheel behind a clear panel. Its armband fits arms 8 to 14 inches and has small holes for ventilation. Both versions secure via Velcro pieces.

Apple iPod shuffle Sport Case $29

Apple | http://store.apple.com

Apple's Sport Case was the first case available for the iPod shuffle, and it's still one of the best for active types. Although the Sport Case is not completely waterproof like the OtterBox case I also recommend here, its dual-lock seal is water-resistant enough to keep your shuffle dry during an accidental submersion—which means it will also protect it from sweat, dust, and dirt, not to mention scratches and drops. A rubber button cover lets you control the shuffle while in the case, and a 4.5-inch extension cable lets you connect headphones with plugs that don't fit into the recessed headphone jack. A permanently attached lanyard lets you wear the Sport Case around your neck—or tie it down in case it happens to take a swim.

BlackCoat T

$20–$45

Koyono | www.koyono.com

A T-shirt in a book about iPod accessories? Sure, it seems odd, but Koyono's line of BlackCoat T shirts make it easy (and inconspicuous) to carry an iPod nano or shuffle when you don't have pockets. Each shirt features a small pocket that stretches across the chest and then down each side; a small vertical zipper in the middle of the chest provides quick access. You slip your nano or shuffle—and perhaps an ID and some cash—down into the side area; whether you're at the gym or out and about, your stuff remains secure, out of the way, and hidden from view. The shirts are available in short- and long-sleeve casual as well as short-sleeve and sleeveless active. (The pockets in BlackCoat T shirts can also accommodate mini and full-size iPods, but the size and weight of these models make them much more noticeable—and less comfortable—when placed in the shirts' pockets.)

Broome Street Leather Case

Standard, $75; mini, $65; shuffle, $45

Kate Spade | www.katespade.com

For those who crave a designer label on their accessories, Kate Spade's Broome Street line of iPod cases is sure to please. Each model is available in one of seven hip color combinations—smooth leather of one color on the outside, textured leather of another inside—with gold-colored metal hardware. A trendy strap lets you tote your iPod like a miniature handbag or clip it onto another bag or a belt. But the Broome Street cases also give your 'Pod some protection: The iPod shuffle and mini versions cover most of your iPod, with the exception of the shuffle's controls and the mini's Click Wheel and screen, respectively; the model for full-size iPods adds a full flip cover to protect the player's face. And what would a designer case be without the label? The shuffle version features an official "kate spade" charm.

Covertec Leather Case   Standard, $40; mini, $35

Covertec I www.covertec.com

I'll get right to the point: Covertec makes the nicest leather flip cases we've seen for the iPod. Smooth, soft, full-grain napa leather; detailed, complementary stitching; excellent construction—it's all here. The versions for full-size iPods include elastic on the sides for a snug fit; a leather strap with a stylish magnetic snap to keep the case closed; a removable belt clip that doesn't leave a protruding stem behind; and a slot for an ID, a credit card, or cash. The mini version closes using two secure snaps on the flip cover and has a nice leather-wrapped belt clip that's permanently attached. All are available in black, black with orange lining, red, or light brown. If you want an attractive, well-made leather case, for yourself or someone else, you can't go wrong with a Covertec—we've purchased them as gifts ourselves.

Crystal Film & 3D Wheel Film Set

Standard, $11; mini, $10; nano, $15

Power Support | www.powersupportusa.com

Many cases leave your iPod's screen and Click Wheel exposed for convenience. The downside to this approach is that it also leaves those surfaces vulnerable to scratches. Power Support's Crystal & 3D Film Set includes two clear, self-adhesive, protective films, one for the screen and the other for the Click Wheel. (The latter covers the center Enter button, as well—the entire Click Wheel is protected without affecting its functionality.) The nano version (called the Crystal Film Cover Set) goes a step further by covering the nano's entire face and back, protecting nearly the entire nano from scratches. Unlike similar products we've seen, Power Support's films are fairly rigid, so they're quite durable and don't leave air bubbles underneath. And if you ever want to take the films off, they can be easily removed without leaving any sticky residue behind.

Delapod Bags

$49–$109

Delarew Designs | www.delapod.net

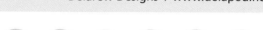

Despite the hundreds of iPod cases on the market, there aren't many stylish yet practical solutions that allow women to bring their iPods along without having to carry an extra item. But Delarew Designs' Delapod line of purses, handbags, and backpacks is a good start. The hip leather bags—six different styles, each available in a number of colors and patterns—provide the usual trimmings, but add an internal pocket with a clear external window through which you can view the screen and access the controls of an iPod stored inside. A handy cable hole lets your headphones escape. (Full-size iPods fit these pockets perfectly on their own; an included set of adapters accommodates mini, nano, and shuffle models.) And in the interest of security, the iPod window is on the side of the bag that sits against your body, so as not to scream "iPod inside!"

Folio for iPod U2 Special Edition $40

Incase | www.goincase.com

If you've got an U2 iPod, you've probably got conflicting desires:
On the one hand, you want to keep it safe—which means putting
it in a case. On the other hand, you want to show it off—what's
the point of getting a Special Edition if it's hidden away? Incase's
Folio is the perfect compromise between solid protection and exhi-
bitionism: A walletlike design featuring black napa leather and red
suede lining keeps your iPod safe from bumps and scratches, while
a clear rear panel displays the Special Edition's most unique feature,
the band's engraved signatures. Sturdy metal snaps keep your iPod
securely inside. For owners of U2 iPods, this is the case to get.

IceWear

$20

Tunewear | www.tunewear.com

There are literally scores of "skin" iPod cases on the market, but we love Tunewear's IceWear. Made of the same silicone used in professional diving masks, the IceWear is clear, flexible yet durable, and very easy to grip; thick, silicone-ridged sides provide additional shock protection. The full-size and mini versions leave the top edge of your iPod exposed so that you can mount accessories such as an iTalk, iTrip LCD, or remote control receiver. Your iPod's screen is also exposed, but the case provides a raised bezel around the screen for added protection. The shuffle version of the IceWear includes covers for both shuffle caps, as well as a short chain to keep the cap attached to the shuffle. If you're looking for some color, the Ice-Wear clearly (no pun intended) isn't the best option, but for overall design and protection, it's one of the best "skins" out there.

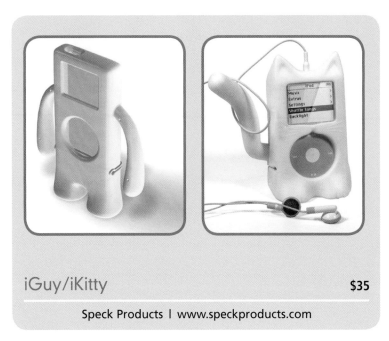

iGuy/iKitty $35

Speck Products | www.speckproducts.com

There are cases, and there are…posable toys posing as cases.
Speck's iGuy and iKitty each cover your full-size or mini iPod in
thick silicone, with a clear plastic insert to protect the iPod's screen;
the Click Wheel remains accessible, and the bottom of the case
flips out of the way to let you place your iPod on a dock. But that's
where the cases end and the toys begin: The iGuy and iKitty just
so happen to look like a person and a cat, respectively. (Think
Gumby, only white—and with an iPod inside.) The iGuy's baseball-
bat-shaped arms and the iKitty's long tail are posable, and the
iGuy's rear even has a, well, *rear*. (Flipping the bottom of the iGuy
open and placing him on a dock results in the most humorous iPod
pose we've seen.) These aren't cases you'll carry around with you,
thanks to their bulk, but for fun at your desk, they don't have much
competition. (Note that the iKitty was not available for the nano at
the time of this writing.)

shuffle Sweats

$19 for pack of two

iMojo | www.imojo.com

The shuffle is perhaps the most popular iPod for exercising, but if your workout clothes don't have a pocket, you need a way to carry it. Apple's lanyard is too bouncy for our tastes, and even the popular armbands can be a hassle. iMojo has come up with a nifty alternative: a traditional terry-cloth sweatband that includes an elastic band to hold your shuffle securely in place. Worn on your forearm, the iMojo puts your iPod within easy reach (and view). It also includes a pair of silicone "cleat wraps" that you can wrap excess headphone cable around—useful for keeping your cables from getting caught on the equipment at the gym. And since shuffle Sweats really are sweatbands, they're machine washable—how many iPod "cases" can make that claim? (Go to the gym more often than you do laundry? The Sweats are sold in packs of two: white/white, black/black, or white/black.)

iPod Armor

4G, color/photo $40; 3G $20

Matias | http://matias.ca/

If you're looking for the ultimate in crushproof protection for your full-size iPod, look no more. A molded aluminum shell that encases the entire player, the Armor also cushions your iPod—and prevents scratches—with a layer of dense foam inside. Openings at the top provide access to the headphone/remote jack and hold switch, and a removable rubber plug at the bottom provides access to the dock connector port. The rest of your iPod's controls and its screen are inaccessible—safely so—making this more of a "press Play and go" case (or, for 3G, 4G, and color/photo iPods, one that you use with Apple's iPod remote). An Armor Clip belt clip is also included. We haven't yet tried to drive our car over our iPod to see if the Armor would keep it safe, but we've been tempted. (Matias also makes a mini version of the iPod Armor; however, that version doesn't offer the same tanklike protection as the full-size model.)

iPod Gear Pouch

Small, $29; large, $35

WaterField Designs | www.sfbags.com

An iPod case is perfect for running around town, but when you travel, you probably bring a number of iPod accessories as well. WaterField Designs' padded ballistic-nylon iPod Gear Pouch aims to make the journey easier—or at least a little more organized— by giving you a place to stash that iPod stuff. The small version (7.8 by 3.8 by 1.2 inches) has several internal pockets designed to hold your iPod, its AC adapter, cables, and earbuds; the large version (10 by 5.3 by 1 inch) adds room for an iPod dock and several other small accessories. Available in a number of colorful trims, the Gear Pouch is perfect for packing your iPod and its accouterments in your suitcase or carry-on.

iSkins $20–$35

iSkin | www.iskin.com

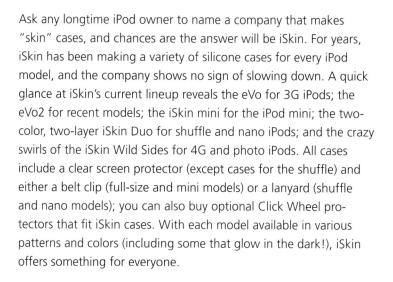

Ask any longtime iPod owner to name a company that makes "skin" cases, and chances are the answer will be iSkin. For years, iSkin has been making a variety of silicone cases for every iPod model, and the company shows no sign of slowing down. A quick glance at iSkin's current lineup reveals the eVo for 3G iPods; the eVo2 for recent models; the iSkin mini for the iPod mini; the two-color, two-layer iSkin Duo for shuffle and nano iPods; and the crazy swirls of the iSkin Wild Sides for 4G and photo iPods. All cases include a clear screen protector (except cases for the shuffle) and either a belt clip (full-size and mini models) or a lanyard (shuffle and nano models); you can also buy optional Click Wheel protectors that fit iSkin cases. With each model available in various patterns and colors (including some that glow in the dark!), iSkin offers something for everyone.

iWood   **$90 and up**

Miniot | www.miniot.com

What do you give the iPod nano or video owner who has everything? How about an elegant, form-fitting case sculpted out of a
single block of wood? That's exactly what you get with the iWood,
which encases an iPod in your choice of maple, mahogany, pear,
walnut, or wengé. (Wood is obtained from FSC-certified, managed
forests.) When closed, only the headphone jack is exposed; when
open, you have full access to the screen, controls, and dock connector port. You can even personalize the iWood by adding a mono-
gram on the front and an engraving inside the lid. There's no belt
clip or lanyard for carrying, and aftermarket headphones with larger
plugs won't fit through the iWood's small headphone jack opening,
but these limitations may be worth it if you enjoy making passers-by
ooh and ah.

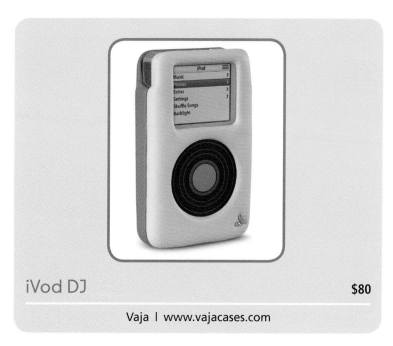

iVod DJ $80

Vaja | www.vajacases.com

Vaja's high-end leather cases are up there with Covertec's on our
list of favorites, but whereas Covertec's offer "executive" styling,
Vaja's tend toward the sporty and hip. Case in point: the iVod DJ.
Like all iVods, this slip-on case features soft, full-grain cowhide
on the outside with a rigid shell underneath for added protection.
But the limited-edition DJ version of the iVod ups the cool quotient
(and the protection) with a use-through Click Wheel cover that
looks just like an LP. (A clear barrier keeps your iPod's screen safe
from harm, so the only part of your iPod that remains exposed
is the top edge.) The DJ is available in literally hundreds of color
combinations, and you can opt to have yours personalized, or even
embossed with your company logo, for an additional fee. Sure, this
is one of the most expensive cases we've seen, but it's also one of
the most unique—and don't forget that each case is handcrafted
and made to order. (Vaja also makes similar cases without the DJ
look for most iPod models.)

iKeychain   **nano, $40 and up; shuffle, $30 and up**

A-1 Quality Products | www.keychainpod.com

The iKeychain is easily the most crush- and bendproof case we've seen for iPod nanos and shuffles. It leaves the nano's Click Wheel and screen, or the shuffle's front and back controls, accessible, but the rest of the iPod's body is completely encased in thick, machined aluminum that the company says can be safely run over with a truck. (We believe it.) And though there are similar-looking metal cases on the market, we like the iKeychain because the front and back pieces are held together by strong magnets instead of screws—the case stays closed even when dropped, but it's easy to get your iPod in and out. The iKeychain's fit and finish are impressive, as is the variety of available styles: The basic models come in a number of anodized colors; for a bit more money, A-1 also offers two-color, multicolor, and chrome-, silver-, and gold-plated models. You can even get your iKeychain custom engraved. (Despite the included ring, we don't recommend using the iKeychain as an actual keychain, as your keys will scratch the iPod's exposed controls and screen.)

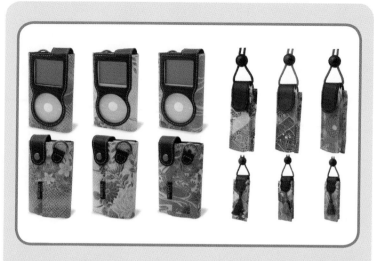

Kimono Case

Standard, $45; shuffle, $23

Power Support | www.powersupportusa.com

Power Support's Kimono Cases are unique in more ways than one. For starters, their Asian-print cotton fabrics—laid over more protective leather—are unlike any other material we've seen in an iPod case. But beyond that, no two cases are alike: Although six patterns are available—three for full-size iPods and three for iPod shuffles—each case is cut individually, so you can be sure that no one else will have quite the same design. The full-size Kimono Case leaves your iPod's Click Wheel and screen accessible, and includes a ring for attaching a lanyard, clip, or keychain. The shuffle version completely encloses your shuffle and includes a matching, adjustable lanyard.

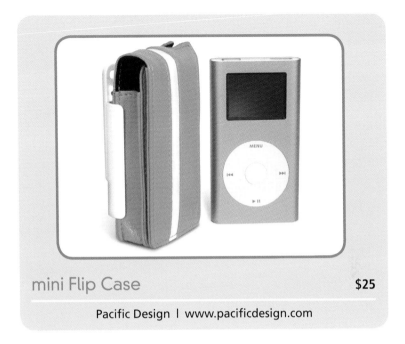

mini Flip Case $25

Pacific Design I www.pacificdesign.com

Pacific Design's Flip Case was one of the first flip cover cases released for the iPod mini, but it's still among our favorites thanks to several thoughtful design touches. Like most flip covers, the Flip Case offers full-body protection while providing easy access to your mini's screen and controls; unlike most, the cover latches closed via small magnets—a design that's thinner than one with straps or snaps and less likely to wear out over time. The headphone jack notch—instead of a hole—is also a clever approach, as it allows you to open and close the flip cover without having to unplug your headphones. Finally, the Flip Case is designed so that your mini's own belt clip can slide right onto the back of the case. We also like the look: The leather-like material and racing-stripe design give the blue, green, and pink models a retro appearance, whereas the new white and black models are more upscale.

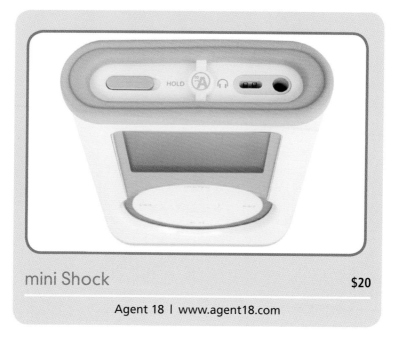

mini Shock $20

Agent 18 | www.agent18.com

Agent 18's mini Shock has it all: attractive design, good protection, and versatility. The two-piece body of the case is made of sturdy white plastic, with thick rubber along the top and bottom to absorb the impact of a fall. Four rubber "bumpers" on the inside of the case provide even more shock protection—your iPod doesn't actually touch the case's plastic sides. Need a way to carry your mini? The case's back panel can be removed and replaced with your iPod mini's belt clip or Apple's Armband accessory without sacrificing protection. And the clear front of the case manages to show off just enough of your iPod mini for its color to shine through. The mini Shock is a nearly perfect compromise between looks, security, and utility.

OtterBox for iPod

**Standard, mini, nano, $50;
shuffle, $30**

Otter Products | www.otterbox.com

Many cases provide scratch and impact protection, but if you want to give your iPod complete shelter from both accidents and elements, OtterBox's iPod cases are the way to go. Each airtight OtterBox envelops your iPod in a waterproof (to 1 meter) case that also provides significant protection against drops, dings, dirt, and dust. Even the headphone jack is sealed off—the case itself plugs into your iPod's headphone jack; you plug your headphones into the OtterBox. (If you're interested in waterproof headphones, Otter-Box recommends those from Swimman; www.swimman.net.) A thick membrane allows you to use your iPod's Click Wheel (or your shuffle's buttons) through the case. The full-size, mini, and nano versions include a removable belt clip; the nano and shuffle versions come with a removable lanyard but also fit in an optional armband. The OtterBox is the most protective iPod case we've seen, and it's the one we use when venturing into environments unforgiving to electronics. (A version for the iPod with video will be available in February 2006.)

Sleevz for iPod

Standard, $21; mini, $19; nano, $18

RadTech | www.radtech.us

People love the iPod's svelte form. They don't like that its shiny surfaces pick up more scratches than a new car in a supermarket parking lot. Thus the dilemma: scratches or a bulky case? RadTech's Sleevz for iPod offer an attractive solution via a form-fitting case made of the company's thin (less than 1 mm thick) Optex microfiber. The suedelike material is tough enough to withstand tearing and scuffing, but soft enough that you can actually use the Sleevz as a polishing cloth for your iPod or your laptop screen. Your iPod remains fully functional while in a Sleevz—a clear plastic window lets you view the screen, the top and bottom edges remain accessible, and embossed areas on the case's face correspond to the controls on your iPod. (The material is thin enough that the controls work through the case.) The Sleevz won't protect your iPod from a fall onto concrete, but when you just want to slip your iPod into your pocket or toss it into a bag, you get scratch protection without bulk.

Showcase $33

Contour Design | www.contourcase.com

One of the few cases that offer serious coverage while still showing off your iPod, the Showcase has thick, rigid rubber edges to protect your iPod from impact (and give you a solid grip), while the case's clear front and back panels let you see your iPod's shiny surfaces and use all the buttons and ports. This combination is enough to win us over, but we also really like the Showcase's more practical features: You can get your iPod in and out of the case fast, thanks to a quick-release latch, and the detachable belt clip doesn't leave an annoying, protruding knob behind. The Showcase for 3G iPods is available in ten different colors; the 4G/photo version is available in black or white. Our recommendation? Anything but white—as well as it matches your iPod, the rubber picks up dirt something crazy.

Silicone Jacket for iPod shuffle $15

Power Support | www.powersupportusa.com

Power Support's Silicone Jacket is one of the most expensive "skin" cases we've seen for the iPod shuffle, but it just may be the best of the lot. Like most skins, it provides an all-over glove of silicone to protect your shuffle, as well as tactile markings over the iPod shuffle's controls to make it easier to locate them by feel. But unlike most similar cases, the Jacket uses thicker, ribbed silicone over the shuffle's Off/Play/Shuffle switch, making it easier to use through the case. The Jacket also uses significantly thicker silicone around the corners of the shuffle, providing better impact protection if you accidentally drop your iPod. Finally, you get covers for both the shuffle's lanyard and USB caps, as well as a plastic belt clip. Sometimes you get what you pay for, and this is a case (no pun intended) in point.

SportGrip for iPod shuffle $10; pack of three, $25

Marware | www.marware.com

Not quite a case and not quite a belt clip, Marware's SportGrip
is nevertheless one of our favorite accessories for the shuffle. It's
basically a silicone rubber holder that fits around the edge of the
shuffle, leaving the front and rear exposed. A small ring lets you
attach the SportGrip to the included carabiner or a lanyard; the
carabiner is perfect for clipping your shuffle onto your bag or belt
loop. Apart from a bit of a cushion on the edges, the SportGrip
doesn't provide the protection of a "real" case, but it's a handy
way to carry your shuffle around. And at only $10 each, or a pack
of three (which includes a lanyard) for $25, the SportGrip is among
the least expensive iPod accessories you'll find. Single SportGrips
are available in ten different colors; three-packs come in black,
white, and gray; or red, blue, and black.

SportSuit Convertible $40

Marware | www.marware.com

Marware's SportSuit Convertible is perfect for active types who want case flexibility, thanks to varying levels of protection and several carrying options. In its most basic state, the Convertible is a neoprene case with rigid sides, rubber grips, and a clear, protective front. Add the removable lid and you get a hard-shell flip case that can also store your earbuds, an ID, and some cash. For carrying, the Convertible comes with a neoprene armband as well as Marware's excellent Multidapt clip system, which can accommodate bike mounts, dash mounts, lanyards, the included belt clip, and more. Full-size and mini versions of the SportSuit Convertible are available in six different colors. The nano version is available in black, blue, or silver and adds a hand strap for easy carrying during exercise; it also uses a slightly different design to accommodate the smaller size of the nano.

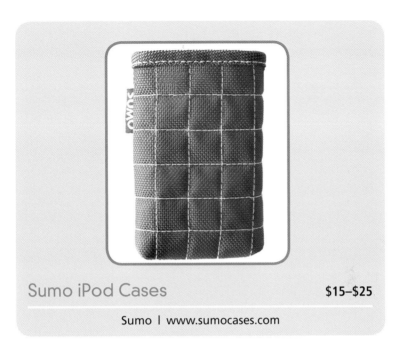

Sumo iPod Cases $15–$25

Sumo | www.sumocases.com

If your iPod is always in a pocket or bag, you probably don't need a case that provides access to the player's screen and Click Wheel. In these situations, a "pouch" case will do just fine, and Sumo's Flap and Sleeve cases are among our favorites. The Quilted and Stripe Sleeve models, identical except for stitching patterns, are constructed of tough ballistic nylon on the outside with a soft lining inside. They stretch to fit any recent full-size iPod and offer protection from scratches and mild bumps while leaving the top edge of the iPod exposed for easy access. The Flap models, available in ballistic nylon or smooth or suede leather, add a snap-closed flap for added protection. A low-profile metal belt clip adorns the back of each case. And despite their excellent quality and attractive design, Sumo's iPod cases are among the least expensive on the market. (Tip: The Sumo Sleeves work great with Nyko's iTop Button Relocator, covered in the Accessories chapter.)

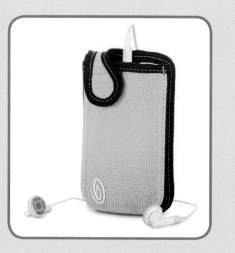

Timbuk2 iPod Case

Standard, $20; mini, $18

Timbuk2 | www.timbuk2.com

If you've always got a bag on your shoulder or a pack on your back, Timbuk2's iPod Case is one of the more practical cases out there. Its padded, plushly lined, ballistic-nylon pouch fits your iPod like a glove and attaches securely to the strap of your bag (or even your belt). You can't access your iPod's Click Wheel or see its screen while using the case, but that's not necessarily a bad thing—if your iPod's dangling from a strap, you want it protected all around. And with 11 color options, you're sure to find one that matches your favorite tote or backpack.

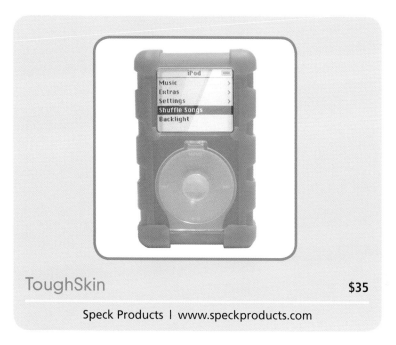

ToughSkin $35

Speck Products | www.speckproducts.com

Speck's ToughSkin, available in five silicone colors, is the SUV of "skin" cases. Unlike most skins, which protect mainly against scratches, the ToughSkin provides significant shock and impact protection, thanks to thick rubber bumpers on the corners and sides—this is one of the few cases in which we felt comfortable dropping an iPod several feet onto the floor. (We don't recommend trying this at home—we're trained professionals.) The ToughSkin also includes a hard plastic screen protector and—on most models— a hard plastic Click Wheel guard that swings out of the way for easy access. A nice touch: The included belt clip can be removed when you aren't using it and doesn't leave an annoying post behind. Speck got nearly everything right with this case—for excellent protection in a case that still provides access to the iPod's controls and connectors, you can't go wrong with the ToughSkin.

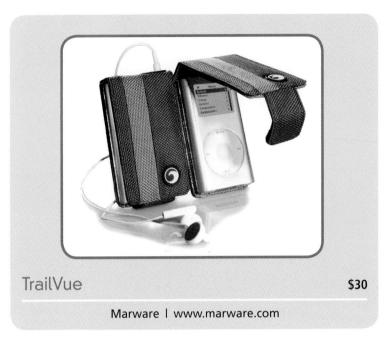

TrailVue $30

Marware | www.marware.com

Unlike most flip cases, which are made of leather, Marware's Trail-
Vue is made of ballistic nylon with rigid inserts in the front and back
to keep your iPod safe from bumps and bruises; a Velcro closure
keeps the flip cover shut. A rare case that looks and feels both rug-
ged *and* sporty, the TrailVue is available in a number of stylish color
combinations—five for full-size iPods and seven for iPod minis, each
with one main color and a "racing stripe" of another. The TrailVue
also comes with one of our favorite features of all Marware cases,
the Multidapt clip. This accessory-mounting system on the back of
the case can be used to connect a number of different accessories,
from the included belt clip to dash mounts to bicycle handlebar
mounts to lanyard attachments, and makes Marware cases some of
the most versatile on the market.

Portable Speakers

The iPod comes with headphones, but sometimes you just want to listen out loud. In this and the next chapter, we'll show you our favorite speaker systems for unwinding (and unwiring) on the road or for sharing your iPod's music with family and friends (and even neighbors) at home. We start with portable systems.

Portable iPod speakers are all the rage, partly because there are so many interesting and stylish models on the market but also because people really like being able to enjoy their music without headphones—no matter where they are. After all, the iPod is a portable player, so it makes sense that you'd want to take your speakers with you, too. We've tested most of what's out there, and these are our favorites; at prices from $40 to $400, you're sure to find something appropriate for your tastes and budget. All can be powered off batteries, and most also offer AC power as an option when you're near an outlet. (In fact, portable speakers are also great for your desk, nightstand, or kitchen counter.) Don't expect the same level of sound quality as provided by the "home" speakers in the next chapter, but if you travel a lot, portable systems likely make up for this limitation in convenience.

Note that all portable speakers included here can be connected to your iPod's headphone jack—either directly or via a "minijack" cable—so all are technically compatible with every iPod. However, some of these speaker systems also provide an iPod cradle that lets you dock your iPod directly; for these systems, our iPod Compatibility Icons indicate which iPod models fit that dock cradle.

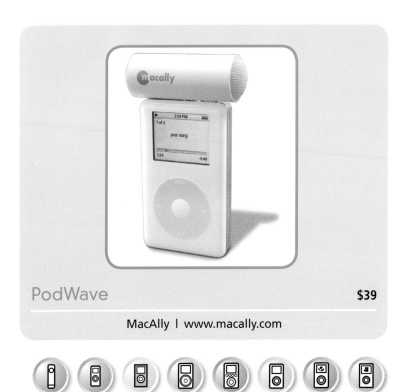

PodWave $39

MacAlly | www.macally.com

If your ultimate goal is portability rather than sound quality, the
PodWave is the miniature speaker system you want. Powered by a
single AA battery, the PodWave plugs directly into your iPod's headphone jack and provides stereo speakers, one at each end; volume
is controlled by your iPod. The resulting sound quality obviously
can't compare with that of the larger systems here—you get no real
bass, slightly tinny output, and fairly low maximum volume—but it's
surprisingly good given the PodWave's ultra-portable size and low
power consumption. The PodWave also lets you take full advantage
of the alarm feature on screened iPods—a handy bonus consider-
ing that the speaker fits into even the smallest bag. (Size: 3.3 inches
long by 1.3 inches in diameter; 1 ounce. Battery: 8 hours, 1 AA.)

i-Station shuffle $50

Logic 3 | www.logic3.com

Most of the speakers covered in this book can be used with an iPod shuffle via a mini-to-mini cable, but if you'd like a system made specifically for your shuffle, Logic 3's i-Station shuffle is our favorite. Loosely resembling its bigger i-Station sibling (also recommended here), this version features a shuffle-only USB dock that charges your iPod as it plays; a USB port on the back of the system lets you sync your shuffle with iTunes, as well. The i-Station shuffle also provides audio line-in and -out jacks (to listen to another source through the speakers or to connect the i-Station to a better audio system at home, respectively). Although the i-Station shuffle is fairly bulky compared to the shuffle itself, and doesn't sound quite as good as the next step up the portable speaker ladder (JBL's On Tour), its shuffle-specific design and syncing features are unique. Look at it this way: For $20 more than Apple's iPod shuffle Dock, you get the same functionality plus some decent speakers. (Size: 7.8 by 5.5 by 1.5 inches; 18 ounces. Battery: 15–20 hours, 4 AAA.)

On Tour   **$100**

JBL | www.jbl.com/home/products/series.aspx?SerId=HMM

Although it doesn't dock with your iPod as many other portable speakers do, the On Tour just may be the best compromise between size and sound quality. Small enough to fit in even the most overstuffed suitcase or laptop bag, and weighing less than a pound, the On Tour still offers impressive detail and good midrange, though—as you might expect—not a lot of bass. The unique sliding cover serves as both protection for the speakers and a stand during use; closing it turns the system off automatically. You'll definitely get better sound by moving up to the more expensive speakers here, but you'll also need more room in your carry-on. And the On Tour—available in white or black—works as well with the iPod shuffle as it does with full-size iPods. (Size: 7 by 3.5 by 1.4 inches; 12 ounces. Battery: ~20 hours, 4 AAA.)

i-Station   **$100**

Logic 3 I www.logic3.com

Among the myriad portable speakers for dockable iPods, Logic 3's
i-Station stands out for providing most of the expected features at a
surprisingly low price. (Imported from the UK, it's been consistently
available for around $85 from Internet retailers such as Amazon.
com.) The i-Station features a folding design similar to that of the
popular (and more expensive) Altec Lansing inMotion iM3 with
sound quality that's nearly as good. It also offers both FireWire
and USB connectivity with your computer (for syncing your iPod); a
"3D" sound processor that aims to provide more spacious sound;
blue ambient lighting; and a subwoofer in the rear. (The sub doesn't
provide any more bass than other similar speaker systems, but it's a
clever design that also acts as a stand.) The included AC adapter also
charges your docked iPod. Even though we think the more expensive models here are worth the extra money, it's nice to know that
you can still get a full-featured system for a bargain price. (Size: 7.8
by 5.5 by 1.5 inches; 18 ounces. Battery: ~15–20 hours, 4 AAA.)

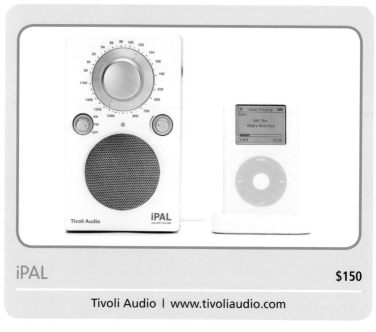

iPAL   **$150**

Tivoli Audio | www.tivoliaudio.com

If you're a radio lover, you'll be hard-pressed to find a better portable speaker solution than the iPAL. (Well, except for the iPAL's bigger sibling, which I'll get to in a few pages.) This attractive, weather-resistant package—our favorite for the beach or backyard—includes one of the best AM/FM radios on the market, with sensitivity and selectivity that outperform that of many expensive tuners and receivers. And, of course, it works great as a speaker for your iPod, connecting via an included cable. Don't be fooled by the fact that the iPAL has only a single speaker—it offers exceptional sound quality that we prefer to that of many portable systems with tiny left/right speakers that are only a few inches apart. A must-have $30 carrying bag holds the iPAL, your iPod, earbuds, and cables. Also consider the PAL, a slightly more rugged version with a rubberized enclosure that's available in a slew of colors. (Size: 3.7 by 3.6 by 3.9 inches; 3.5 pounds. Battery: 15–20 hours, rechargeable.)

mm50 $150

Altec Lansing's inMotion iM3 is likely the most popular portable iPod speaker system on the market, so it's only natural to compare similar products with it. And we think Logitech outdid the iM3 with the mm50. Like the iM3, the mm50 includes a wireless remote, charges your docked iPod when connected to AC power, and syncs your iPod with your computer via Apple's dock connector cable. But whereas the mm50 is only slightly bigger than the iM3, it offers better sound, a sturdier build, and a rechargeable internal battery. Best of all, it's less expensive, making it a great deal all around. (Size: 12.8 by 3.8 by 1.4 inches; 23 ounces. Battery: 10 hours, internal rechargeable.)

iBoom   **$150**

Digital Lifestyle Outfitters | www.dlodirect.com

What do you get when you cross an iPod with a boom box? An iBoom, of course. Which is to say, a 20-watt portable sound system that may not blow you away with its sound quality but *will* let you listen to your iPod loud and proud on the go. And when you get tired of your own music, you can enjoy your local radio station via the built-in digital FM tuner. Relive the '80s by carrying the iBoom on your shoulder, or use the small carry slot. I recommend the latter, if only because you won't look like a dork, but even better is the $30 BoomBag—a form-fitting, padded carrying case that protects the iBoom while offering an easy way to carry it. (Size: 12.5 by 8 by 5 inches; 5 pounds. Battery: ~30 hours, 6 D.)

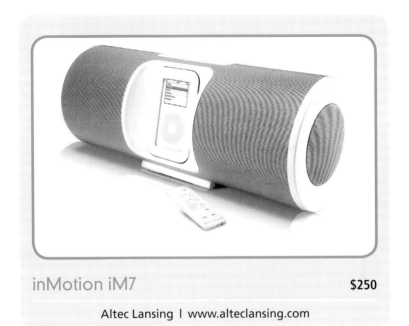

inMotion iM7 $250

Altec Lansing | www.alteclansing.com

The inMotion iM7 may not fit in your bag like other portable speaker systems, but those systems can't hold a candle to the iM7 in terms of sound quality. Whether you're listening out loud outside or at more reserved levels indoors, the iM7 provides impressive audio in an eye-catching package. Treble and bass—yes, actual bass—are adjustable via the included remote, which also lets you control playback and volume. If your iPod can project photos or video, the iM7's built-in composite- and S-video jacks let you connect the system to your TV for easy viewing. And did I mention that the AC adapter works with most wall power sockets around the world? The iM7 proves that you don't have to give up great sound to get a speaker system you can take with you. The optional Shoulder Harness and Shoulder Pack ($50 each) provide several ways to carry the iM7 around besides its built-in handle. (Size: 16.8 inches long by 6.3 inches in diameter; 11 pounds. Battery: 8–10 hours, 8 D batteries.)

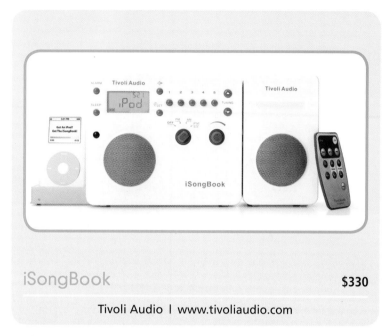

iSongBook   **$330**

Tivoli Audio | www.tivoliaudio.com

Tivoli's original SongBook is widely considered one of the best portable radios on the market, with a stellar tuner that works around the
world; ten presets; a backlit digital display that doubles as an alarm
clock; and pristine, if bass-light, sound quality. It's even weather
resistant, so you can take it to the beach. But Tivoli went above and
beyond for the *i*SongBook, by adding a detachable second speaker
with a retractable 6-foot cable as well as an iPod dock base. The
base flips up and into the body of the iSongBook when not in use,
and you can detach the second speaker for easier packing (or leave
it at home if your suitcase is getting cramped). Finally, an included
remote lets you control both your iPod and the iSongBook itself, and
an optional carrying bag makes it easy to tote the whole package.
If you love your iPod *and* the radio, what more could you ask for?
(Size: 11 by 6.3 by 2.3 inches, 3.2 pounds, including second speaker.
Battery: 10–15 hours, 6 AA; AC adapter can charge rechargeable
batteries.)

Model Twelve   **$400**

Cambridge SoundWorks | www.cambridgesoundworks.com

If you insist on top-notch sound wherever you go, and you're willing to use the term *portable* loosely, the Model Twelve provides a complete stereo system—integrated amplifier, stereo speakers, and subwoofer—in a "luggable" package. (We call it *transportable*.) The case, approximately the size of a small carry-on suitcase, also serves as the system's subwoofer. Sound quality and volume level are head and shoulders above those of other portable systems we've tested—and of most of the home systems, for that matter—and thanks to four inputs and a tape-out, the Model Twelve can serve as a home stereo when you're not out and about. It can be powered off AC, DC, or an optional battery pack, and the sturdy case has room for your iPod and cables. Alas, at 30 pounds, all this quality and flexibility come at a hefty (no pun intended) price. (Size: 17.5 by 10.5 by 7.5 inches; 30 pounds with battery. Battery: $50 option, 8–12 hours, rechargeable.)

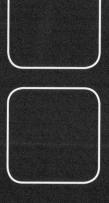

Home Speakers

In the previous chapter, we covered portable iPod speakers; in this one, we tackle "home" systems, which differ from portable speakers in several ways. For starters, they require AC power, so you can't use them on the go. But they also tend to sound a lot better than comparably priced portable speakers. Part of the reason for this is that the manufacturer doesn't have to worry about power consumption (read: battery life) and can spend money on audio quality rather than miniaturization. But it's also because these systems tend, with a few exceptions, to use separate left and right speakers (satellites) and a subwoofer, so you get better stereo separation and bass.

All the speaker systems in this chapter provide their own amplification—you just hook up your iPod and press Play. Some models, such as those from iHome, Bose, and Klipsch, include an iPod dock base for an easy connection. (For these speakers, our iPod model icons refer to the system's docking compatibility.) However, most simply use a standard audio "mini" cable that plugs into your iPod's headphone jack or the line-out jack of an iPod dock (such as one of those recommended in the General Accessories chapter). All but Bose's SoundDock can also be connected to your computer or to the audio output of Apple's AirPort Express for more listening options.

(Note that if you've already got a good home stereo, you don't need to buy a home speaker system; you can simply hook your iPod up to your existing stereo. We recommend some great accessories for doing so in the General Accessories chapter.)

Digital Fidelity One $60

RSL | www.rogersoundlabs.com

Compared with most of the iPod accessories out there, the Digital Fidelity One may seem a bit, well, plain. But don't let the DFO's pedestrian looks fool you—when the folks at Rogersound Labs decided to make an inexpensive speaker system, they also decided to focus on sound, not appearance. The audible results will floor you—you simply won't find better sound for the cost of a few CDs. You also get features rarely found at this price, such as digital volume controls and super-solid construction. As someone who's a stickler for good audio quality, I often find it difficult to recommend inexpensive speakers, which are usually an exercise in compromise. But the Digital Fidelity One is a different story: If you don't mind the early-'90s looks, this is a well-rounded, enjoyable system.

Creature II $100

JBL | www.jbl.com/home/products/series.aspx?SerId=HMM

The first thing you'll notice about this system is its iPod-matching white and chrome surfaces. But you'll soon forget the speakers' skin tones as you become captivated by their shape: The appropriately named Creature II features a subwoofer and tiny satellites that look more like ghouls than gear. Even more impressive is the sound quality for the price—people are frequently shocked by the audio put out by this relatively small system. It won't play as loud as bigger systems, and it emphasizes detail over bass, but the Creature II provides some of the best bang-for-the-buck sound of any system we've tested, and a combination of sound quality and killer design unmatched in the under-$100 market. Treble and bass controls let you fine-tune the sound, and nifty touch-sensitive buttons on the right satellite let you adjust the volume. And if you're tired of white, the Creature II is also available in gloss black, matte silver, and matte red.

Z-4i $100

Logitech | www.logitech.com

Like the Creature II from JBL, the Logitech Z-4i is an attractive, good-sounding speaker system that—at street prices—comes in well under the magical $100 price point. Instead of the other-worldly design of the Creature II, the Z-4i takes a more traditional aesthetic approach. But that's not to say the Z-4i is unattractive: Its sleek, white-and-silver styling is a perfect match for white iPods (as well as Apple's white iMacs, iBooks, and eMacs). And you can even remove the satellites' cast-metal stands and mount the speakers on the wall. The svelte sub, just 9 inches square, provides impressive, if boomy, bass for its size, and the handy controller puts a volume knob, a bass control, a second audio input, and a headphone jack in easy reach. We (ever-so-slightly) prefer the sound of the Creature II to that of the Z-4i, but the Logitech system's convenient controller and setup flexibility make it just as appealing an option.

ProMedia Ultra 2.0

$100

Klipsch | www.klipsch.com

If you're cramped for space, or if you just want to easily move your audio system around the house, the ProMedia Ultra 2.0 is just the ticket—the "2.0" means no subwoofer, leaving you with just 10.5-inch-tall left and right speakers. This 30-watt system's 1-inch tweeters and dual 2.5-inch drivers produce clear highs, solid mid-range, and loads of volume, while still providing good bass despite the lack of a subwoofer. Dual inputs (one on the front of the right speaker and one on the back) let you connect the ProMedia Ultra 2.0 to both your computer and your iPod, and bass and volume controls on the right speaker let you adjust levels to your taste. We don't know of a better-sounding small system, especially at this price.

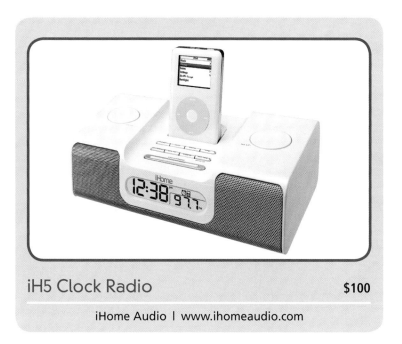

iH5 Clock Radio $100

iHome Audio | www.ihomeaudio.com

When you think about it, an "iPod alarm clock" is an obvious product: People like to wake up to music, so why shouldn't it be their favorite music? Yet it took years before such a product was released. Thankfully, iHome Audio got it just about right with the iH5. By combining the things most likely to be on an iPod owner's nightstand, desk, or kitchen counter—a clock, a radio, and iPod speakers—the iH5 is a killer little system. Truth be told, we didn't expect a lot from a product that tried to do so much for $100, but the clock's display is large and easy to read, sound quality and radio reception are quite good, and your iPod is even charged while docked. When you consider how much it would cost to get similar functionality via separate products, the iH5 is a no-brainer. And it looks pretty good, too. (An optional wireless remote control—a must-have accessory, in our opinion—is $20.)

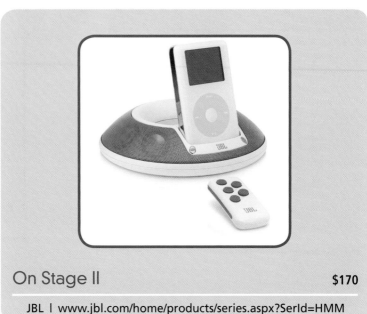

On Stage II $170

JBL I www.jbl.com/home/products/series.aspx?SerId=HMM

Need good sound in a tight space? The On Stage II places four small speakers in an iPod-matching, 7-inch, doughnut-shaped design. You won't get a lot of bass, but the sound is otherwise impressive—especially the treble detail and the surprisingly expansive soundstage. Since it connects to your iPod's dock connector port, the On Stage not only grabs the port's higher-quality audio, but also charges your iPod while docked. And if you connect Apple's dock connector cable to the port on the back of the On Stage, your iPod is synced with your computer, as well. The On Stage II includes a wireless remote so that you can control your iPod and the system volume from across the room. (If you're within arm's reach, you can instead use the touch-sensitive volume buttons.) The original On Stage I, which doesn't include the remote control, is still available for $160.

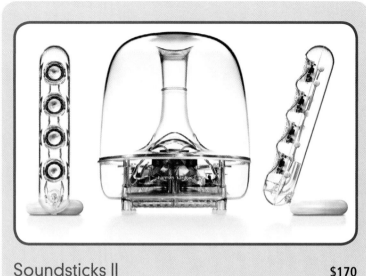

Soundsticks II $170

Harman Kardon | www.harmankardon.com

If JBL's Creature II is otherworldly in its design, Harman Kardon's Soundsticks II system is positively underwaterish. With a sub that looks like a new species of jellyfish and four-driver satellites that will look right at home next to your aquarium, this system certainly won't go unnoticed on your desk. The good news is that the sound quality will also attract attention, with excellent detail and good overall balance. You don't get some of the extra features of other systems in this price range, such as a headphone jack or multiple inputs, but given how much better the system looks, that just might be an acceptable tradeoff. As with the Creature II (JBL and Harman Kardon are divisions of the same parent company), you control the volume via touch-sensitive buttons on the right satellite. The only problem with the Soundsticks II is that it may end up taking more of your precious desk space than expected—you'll be tempted to put the sub where you can see it.

FX6021   **$250**

Altec Lansing I www.alteclansing.com

If we had to pick our favorite "computer" speaker system, Altec
Lansing's FX6021 would be tough to beat out. With a street price
far lower than its $250 list, the FX6021 costs half as much as many
competing systems, yet it provides some of the best sound of any
computer speaker system we've heard. And it doesn't just sound
good: The Power Mac G5–inspired design is easy on the eyes, and
the six-driver satellites can be removed from their weighted bases
and mounted on the wall to save space. A wired controller lets you
adjust volume, bass, and treble, as well as connect headphones and
a second audio input without having to fiddle behind the sub; a
wireless remote provides the same audio adjustments from across
the room. If the FX6021 had a built-in iPod dock, it just might be
the perfect midrange speaker system. For now, you'll just have to
provide your own dock.

SoundDock $300

Bose | www.bose.com

There's no doubt that Bose's SoundDock is pricey—you can get better sound from the less expensive FX6021 on the previous page—and with no auxiliary input or computer-sync features, the SoundDock is fairly limited in its functionality. But it's tough to find the same room-filling sound in a package this small and easy to use. You simply plop your iPod into the SoundDock's cradle and press Play; your iPod is charged while you enjoy the surprisingly rich and spacious audio. The included wireless remote lets you control both volume and playback, and several cradle inserts are included to fit various sizes of dockable iPods.

iFi $400

Klipsch | www.klipsch.com

Put simply, Klipsch's iFi is the best sounding iPod-specific speaker system on the market—nothing else really comes close. It's also the first "home" system designed specifically for the iPod; you can't use it to sync your iPod to your computer, but you get more power and higher-quality components than you'll find in traditional computer speakers. The iFi's Control Dock holds (and charges) dockable iPods and includes both volume and bass controls; a wireless remote lets you control volume and iPod playback. The system's impressive sub includes a 200-watt amplifier that powers the sub as well as the Reference Series RSX-3 satellites—the same speakers that the company sells separately for home use. How good is it? The iFi's full, rich sound puts it in the same league as many good home stereo systems; and although you could put together a home stereo that sounds better, you'd be hard-pressed to do so for $400, including the convenience of the dock base and remote control.

iCub

$750 (plus satellite speakers)

Focal-JMlab I www.focal.tm.fr/home/en/sibco/index.htm

For the audiophile iPod owner who has everything, there's Focal-JMlab's iCub. Expensive? Sure. But this is one sweet combo: an 8-inch subwoofer; three BASH amplifiers (a 150-watt unit for the sub, one 75-watt unit for each satellite); and a 20-bit digital-to-analog converter (DAC). Just plug in your own satellite speakers and a source—you can connect up to two analog devices (such as an iPod and a CD player) as well as a digital source (such as Apple's AirPort Express or a CD player with digital output)—and you've got a full-blown home stereo system. You even get a remote control for system volume. And all of this functionality fits in an attractive (and space-saving—only 13-by-12-by-12-inch) package that looks more like a designer Nintendo GameCube than a home audio system. Thanks to Focal-JMlab's audiophile roots, when paired with a quality set of satellites the iCub outperforms pretty much any home stereo you'll buy at your local electronics superstore, and its compact size and attractive appearance will definitely make it a better fit for your decor.

Headphones

As cute and identifiable as the iPod's stock white earbuds are, they're no match for the quality of sound the iPod can produce. So even though a case is the first accessory many iPod owners will buy, a good pair of headphones is quite possibly the best bang-for-the-buck upgrade—after all, you'll get a good amount of additional enjoyment out of your iPod if your music sounds more musical.

The good news for headphone upgraders is that there are scores of great headphones available. The bad news is that it can be difficult to find the good models among the hundreds of mediocre ones. Being headphone aficionados, we've chosen some of our favorites here. Among our choices, you're sure to find something for everyone, no matter which style they prefer: earbuds or "canalphones," lightweight or full-size, wireless or noise-canceling. If a model is included here, it sounds great for its type (and price). In other words, this chapter will help you get the best cans (that's hip slang for headphones) for your cash.

(Note that all headphones included here will sound great when used directly from your iPod's own headphone jack. There are a good number of other excellent headphones—especially full-size models—that we didn't include because they require more power to sound good than a portable player can provide.)

MX 500

K 14 P

$20

$26

Sennheiser
www.sennheiserusa.com

AKG
www.akg.com

If you like earbuds but are looking for better ones than those that
came with your iPod, there aren't many choices—after all, Apple's
earbuds are better than most, and earbuds can only do so much.
That said, AKG's K 14 P and Sennheiser's MX 500 are the cream of
the earbud crop. Both provide better overall sound, especially when
it comes to treble detail, and include an inline control for adjusting
volume when your iPod's in your pocket. And both come in iPod-
matching colors: the MX 500 in white and silver, and the K 14 P in
black and silver.

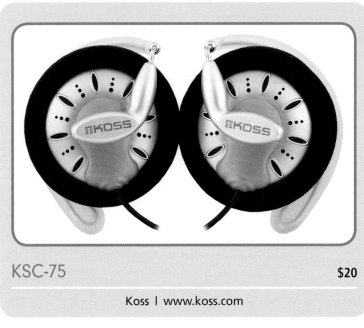

KSC-75 $20

Koss | www.koss.com

Finding the right headphones for exercising can be a challenge, but Koss's KSC-75 may just be the perfect solution. Instead of using a headband, the lightweight earpieces hook onto each ear via a comfortable, rubber-covered clip (which means they're also great for people who don't want to mess up their hair). What's more, the KSC-75 are the best-sounding headphones we've heard for under $30, offering impressive bass response as well as good detail and midrange. And with their silver finish and retro design, they don't look like most cheap models. You won't find a better replacement for your iPod's 'buds for about the cost of a CD.

Headphones

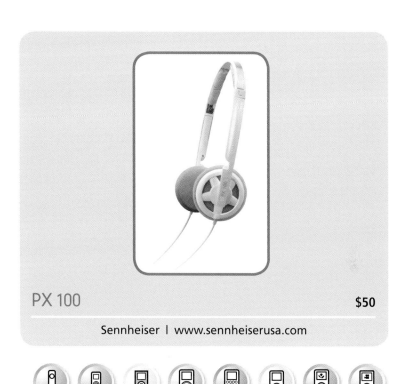

PX 100

$50

Sennheiser | www.sennheiserusa.com

Remember when most portable cassette and CD players came with cheap, over-the-head headphones that sounded as bad as they looked? Oh, how far lightweight headphones have come. The PX 100 are quite possibly the best ever of this genre, featuring great sound quality, all-day comfort, and a design that allows them to fold up like a pair of eyeglasses for travel. (A handy hard-shell case is included.) And with the release of a new white, silver, and gray model, even style-conscious iPod owners will have a hard time resisting. Fifty bucks may seem like a lot to spend on this type of headphones when you're used to getting them for free, but trust us on this one. Your ears will thank you.

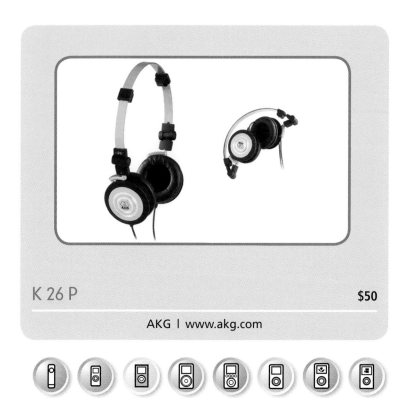

K 26 P $50

AKG I www.akg.com

AKG's K 26 P headphones don't sound *quite* as good as Sennheiser's PX 100—you don't get the same impressive midrange and overall balance—and they aren't quite as comfortable, either. But they nevertheless stand out for offering things that are *very* difficult to find in small, lightweight headphones: a closed design and killer bass. The K 26 P's small leather earpieces block a good amount of external sound, and their bass response will leave you wondering if there's a subwoofer hidden somewhere in the room. Best of all, the K 26 P fold up to fit into the included travel pouch. If you want to feel the impact of your rock, rap, and hip-hop, but don't like carrying around a set of full-size headphones, these are the cans for you. (An iPod-matching white version, the K 27 i, should be available soon.)

Headphones

SR 60

$69

Grado | www.gradolabs.com

At first glance, Grado's SR 60 headphones look like something you might find in your grandparents' garage. But one listen and you'll be willing to overlook the SR 60's homely appearance. Often described as the "gateway to audiophile sound," these cans sound better than many models that cost twice as much—their punchy but natural sound will floor first-time listeners. The SR 60 is the perfect solution for those searching for a set of full-size, high-end home headphones that won't break the bank. However, they aren't ideal for portable use, thanks to their thick cables and loose fit.

Headphones

DT 231 $70

Beyerdynamic | www.beyerdynamic.com

Beyerdynamic may not be a household name for most iPod users, but if you're looking for a set of full-size, closed headphones, you owe it to your ears (and your wallet) to check out the DT 231. These plain-looking headphones consistently amaze us with their balanced sound, and thanks to plush earpads and a spring-loaded headband, they're also among the most comfortable headphones we've used. It would be tough to find better overall sound and comfort in a closed design for under $100, and we like them better than many headphones that cost much more than that.

Headphones

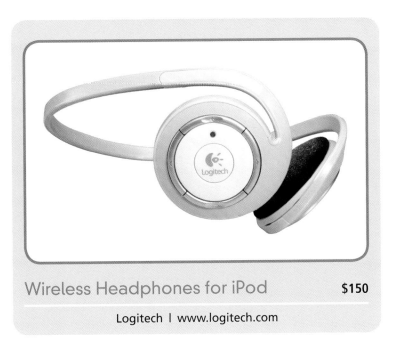

Wireless Headphones for iPod   **$150**

Logitech | www.logitech.com

Although not the most comfortable headphones on the market—
or the best sounding—Logitech's descriptively named Wireless
Headphones for iPod are possibly the most convenient. Attach a
small Bluetooth transmitter to the top of your mini, 3G, 4G, or
photo/color iPod, and the behind-the-head-style headphones let
you listen to your music wirelessly and static-free. Best of all, you
can control playback directly from the right earpiece, which provides
play/pause, forward, back, and volume buttons—your iPod remains
safely in your bag or pocket. You charge the transmitter and headphones via the included AC adapter.

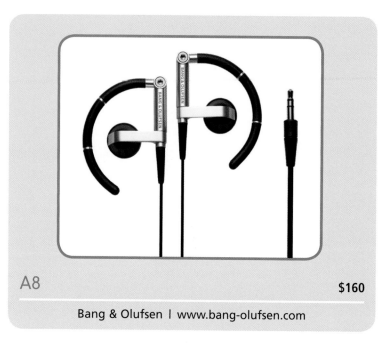

A8 $160

Bang & Olufsen | www.bang-olufsen.com

Let's get this out of the way: You can find better sound quality in a different set of headphones for the money you'll spend on Bang & Olufsen's A8. But it probably won't look as good—the A8's anodized-aluminum bodies are guaranteed to earn envious looks from passersby. They're also surprisingly sturdy, and the earbud/earclip hybrid earpieces are quite comfortable, thanks to a super-adjustable design and light weight. Because the actual headphone drivers use an earbud design, you won't get a lot of bass, but you do get good detail. And B&O includes some useful accessories: a 2-meter extension cable for use at home and an attractive leather travel case. For the style- or design-conscious iPod owner, the A8 is almost a status symbol.

Headphones

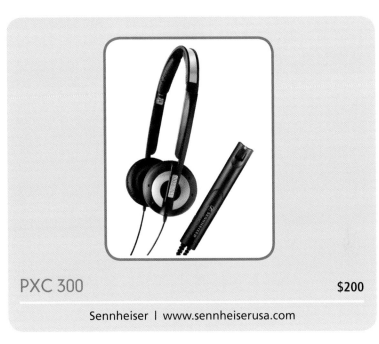

PXC 300   **$200**

Sennheiser | www.sennheiserusa.com

If you're not a fan of sticking things way down in your ear canals (see the next page), your only real choice for travel listening is a set of noise-canceling headphones, which sample outside sound and then pipe in an inverse audio signal to "cancel out" a good amount of monotonous noise, such as airplane engines and train rumblings. Although Bose may be the most well known name in this market, we like the PXC 300, which offer slightly better sound quality than Bose's popular Quiet Comfort II for a lot mess money. The PXC 300 aren't quite as comfortable as the plus QCII, but they're still easy to wear for hours at a time. And when folded up in the included hard travel case, the PXC 300 take up less than half the space in your bag.

Headphones

In-Ear-Canal Headphones

In-ear-canal headphones—also known as *canalphones*—are all the rage among iPod owners, and for good reason: When you stick these earplug-like headphones down into your ear canals, the noise of the outside world is blissfully blocked—you get better noise isolation than even the best noise-canceling headphones can provide. At the same time, the sound quality produced by these miniature marvels is nothing short of amazing. You'll hear things in your music that you never even knew were there. This combination of isolation and sound quality has made canalphones the accessory of choice for many a frequent flyer and urban commuter. (Although, for obvious reasons, we don't recommend wearing them while walking down a dark alley, alone, at night.)

That said, before you rush out and buy a set of canalphones, a few caveats are in order. The first is that if you don't like wearing earplugs, you won't like wearing any of these headphones—after all, they're basically earplugs that reproduce music. The second is that in order to realize their potential, you need to make sure that their earpieces get a solid seal in your ears. Without this seal, the sound is thin and disappointing, and for some people, getting such a seal takes practice. Finally, because they sit in your ear canals and don't move much air, canalphones don't give you the same visceral "kick" at the low end as many larger headphones do. Bass is there, and it's generally excellent—tight, extended, and accurate. But don't expect the kind of thumpin', boomin' bass notes you'll get with some of the larger headphones we've recommended. (If you're looking for more bass, the FS1 canalphones have the most of the models listed here.)

Still with us? Good. On the next few pages, you'll see some of our favorite canalphones, in order of increasing price. At least for the models listed here, you get what you pay for: More money gets you better sound or better features—or both. But all are stellar performers; how much you should spend depends on how picky

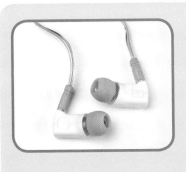

super.fi 3 Studio
$100

Ultimate Ears
www.ultimateears.com

ER-6i
$130

Etymotic Research
www.etymotic.com

FS1
$150

Future Sonics/XtremeMac
www.xtrememac.com

your ears are and at what bit rates you you rip your music—the higher the bit rate, the more you'll appreciate the higher-end models. (We were tempted to include several less expensive models here, but the truth is that our "entry-level" model, Ultimate Ears' $100 super.fi 3 Studio, is so much better than the popular models selling for $30 to $50 that it's worth saving up.) Whether you opt for one of the models recommended here or for one of the other offerings from these manufacturers, there's never been a better time to be a fan of in-ear-canal headphones.

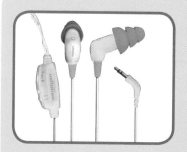

inMotion iM716
$200

Altec Lansing
www.alteclansing.com

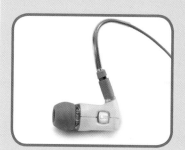

super.fi 5 Pro
$250

Ultimate Ears
www.ultimateears.com

ER-4P
$270

Etymotic Research
www.etymotic.com

E4c
$299

Shure
www.shure.com

Headphones

UE-5c $550

Ultimate Ears | www.ultimateears.com

You're probably thinking, "What? $550 for headphones for my iPod???" Fair enough. But if you do a lot of traveling, trust us: It's worth it. The UE-5c are basically canalphones like those covered in the previous few pages, but two things set them apart. The first is that they use a dual-driver design—one driver for high frequencies, one for low—for better overall sound. The second is that whereas most canalphones include a number of different-sized silicone and foam "tips," one of which hopefully fits your ear canals, the UE-5c's are custom-made for your ears, and your ears only. You go to an audiologist and get impressions of your ear canals made; a few weeks later, your new custom canalphones show up at your door. (You even get to choose the earpiece and cable color, and the cable length.) Do these custom-fit canalphones really sound better than the Shure E4c, which sell for $250 less? A bit, yes. But the real advantage of the UE-5c is in comfort—you can wear them for an entire cross-country flight without the "raw ear" feeling you sometimes get with standard canalphones. A few "test" trips to Hawaii and we were sold.

Headphones

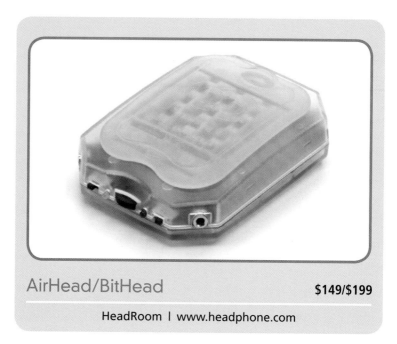

AirHead/BitHead $149/$199

HeadRoom | www.headphone.com

Although the headphones recommended here are efficient enough to be used directly from your iPod, many high-end headphones are not. If you're a fan of power-hungry 'phones, or an audiophile who rips your music at high bit rates (or, even better, using Apple Lossless), then you're just the sort of person who will appreciate a portable headphone amplifier. Unlike the iPod's built-in headphone jack, a good headphone amp such as HeadRoom's AirHead or BitHead will be able to drive even the most inefficient headphones. But we're not just talking volume here; we mean better audio quality, as well—deep, tight bass, natural midrange, and improved clarity. And HeadRoom's amplifiers include the company's special crossfeed circuitry, which makes listening to headphones more like listening to speakers or live music. Combine your iPod, an AirHead, high-end headphones, and high-quality music files, and you've got a killer portable listening system. (The BitHead includes a USB input and digital-to-analog converter that let you use the amp as an external sound card for your computer.)

Complete HeadCase Headphone Bag $89

HeadRoom | www.headphone.com

Know someone who always carries full-size headphones around? Help them treat their 'phones right with a good bag. HeadRoom's fully padded Complete HeadCase fits even the largest headphones comfortably. It also provides a handy see-through (and operate-through) compartment for an iPod, and has room for additional cables, accessories, and—for the audiophile types—a portable headphone amplifier. It even includes handy cable-routing holes to let your big-headphones fan hook everything up nice and tidy-like.

Headphones

Auto Accessories

If you've got a car or truck, you probably spend a good amount of time in it, and you likely spend much of *that* time listening to music. So it's only natural that you want to listen to your iPod while motoring about. A lucky few have a newer car with iPod integration, or at least a line-in jack, built in. For the rest of us, here are some of the best products for playing your iPod through your car's stereo; keeping your iPod running through the longest road trip; and holding your iPod in place as you travel over speed bumps and potholes.

IceLink Plus $199

Dension | www.densionusa.com

Tired of fiddling with tape adapters, FM transmitters, and iPod remotes? Dension's IceLink Plus lets you replace your car's CD changer—it's compatible with dozens of different car makes and models—with an iPod. Since your iPod is wired in directly, the IceLink offers far better sound quality than you get with FM transmitters or cassette adapters, and it powers and charges the iPod, too. If your steering wheel has audio controls, you can even use those to control your iPod. Instead of selecting different discs in the changer, you use your stereo's disc controls to choose from five iPod playlists. (Or flip the iPod into manual mode and control it yourself.) You can have the IceLink Plus professionally installed so that your iPod is mounted in your glove compartment or on your dashboard. However, we found that the IceLink's true calling is really as a CD-changer replacement; we pulled our old changer out of our trunk and replaced it with an iPod mini, and driving has never been the same since.

Drive+Play $200

Harman Kardon | www.harmankardon.com

Harman Kardon's Drive+Play is similar to Dension's IceLink Plus in that it fully integrates your iPod into your car stereo system. However, it bests the IceLink in at least one department by offering the best in-car interface we've seen. Plug the Drive+Play's dock connector cable into your dockable iPod, and your iPod's interface appears on the Drive+Play's five-line, backlit LCD display—you have full access to all playlists, artists, albums, and songs via a five-button, rotating controller that mimics the iPod's own Click Wheel. The Drive+Play connects directly to any car stereo with an auxiliary input jack using a standard audio cable, or to most stereos with a CD changer connecter via an optional third-party adapter. (The system also has a built-in FM transmitter for those who want the screen and controller but would rather avoid a more complex installation.) Like the IceLink, it even charges your iPod while connected. The only drawback is that everyone who rides in your car will want to play with it.

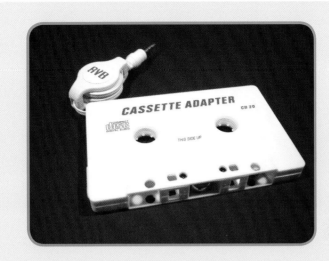

AVB Cassette Adapter for iPod   **$10**

AVB | www.avbusa.com

If your car has a cassette player, the easiest way to hook up your iPod—and one that will generally provide better sound quality than an FM transmitter—is a cassette adapter. This accessory looks like a standard audiocassette but includes a cable that plugs into your iPod's headphone jack; you switch your stereo to Tape mode and your iPod plays through the adapter. Although we've had some issues with compatibility—some car stereos don't get along with some adapters—most work fine, and they're all relatively inexpensive. But AVB's Cassette Adapter for iPod is one of our favorites because of a simple "Why doesn't everybody do that?" feature: Its 3-foot cable automatically retracts into a small reel, much like the well-known Zip-Linq retractable computer cables. So the cable is only as long as it needs to be during use; and when you're not using it, you don't have stray cables all over your car.

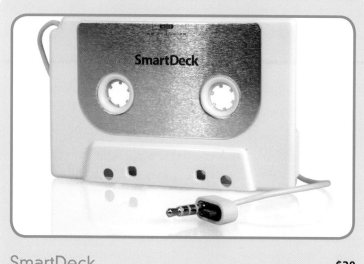

SmartDeck $30

Griffin Technology | www.griffintechnology.com

Remote-jack version

Dock-connector version

Like any run-of-the-mill cassette adapter, Griffin's SmartDeck allows you to listen to your iPod via your car's cassette deck. But the SmartDeck is limited to iPods with remote functionality (via either a remote jack or dock connector), and for good reason: Special sensing technology in the adapter allows you to use your car stereo's controls—including those mounted on the steering wheel—to control iPod playback: play, skip tracks, and pause/stop. Switching to the radio or CD pauses your iPod, and the SmartDeck automatically adjusts your iPod's volume level for the best audio quality—no more fiddling with the volume control to find the "perfect" level. You get much of the functionality of expensive iPod auto adapters at a fraction of the price.

flexDock mini $50

TEN Technology | www.tentechnology.com

TEN Technology's flexDock mini offers iPod mini users one of
the most convenient ways to mount their player in the car. The
flexDock's "cigarette lighter" base plugs into your car's accessory
jack and provides a 7-inch arm with a cradle to hold your iPod mini
(along with power to charge it). The flexible arm places your mini at
an accessible height, while the locking cradle holds it firmly in place.
You can then connect an FM transmitter to your iPod or connect an
audio cable, FM transmitter, or the included cassette adapter to the
flexDock's two-level audio output. And although the flexDock's gray
finish may not match your iPod, it's likely to be a good match for
most car dashboards and consoles. (Although TEN doesn't officially
advertise the flexDock as being compatible with the iPod nano, we
found that the combination works quite well.)

iSqueez $10

Griffin Technology | www.griffintechnology.com

Some of the best products are also the simplest. The iSqueez is simply an iPod stand for your car's cup holder—nothing more, nothing less. But Griffin got the details right. The bottom is just under 3 inches in diameter but compresses to fit into smaller cup holders. The top is cleverly designed to securely fit all iPod models—full-size in one direction, mini and nano (and, loosely, even the shuffle) in the other. It doesn't use suction cups as similar products do, so it's easy to put your iPod in and get it out, and the soft foam won't leave any scratches on your car or your player. A small notch in each side of the iSqueez accommodates the cable of a car charger or other dock-connector accessory. If you've got an extra cup holder, the iSqueez provides the perfect grip, and, at only $10, it's a bargain.

Universal Car Mount $20

Nyko I www.nyko.com

If you're short on cup holders, Nyko's Universal Car Mount gives you a clever iPod holder that mounts on either your air vents or your dashboard. The bottom of the Car Mount cradles your full-size or mini iPod—leaving room for a car charger—while a spring-loaded rear bumper and locking arms hold your player securely in place. Press a button on the top of the Mount and the arms release. The unit mounts using either an included adhesive base or plastic-covered metal clips that grab the slats on your car's air vents. The Car Mount leaves the top of your iPod unobstructed so that you can use a top-mounted FM transmitter or remote control.

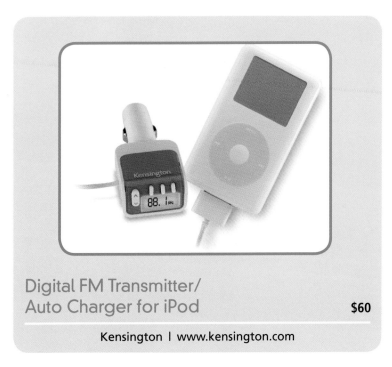

Digital FM Transmitter/
Auto Charger for iPod $60

Kensington I www.kensington.com

Because FM transmitters usually suffer from interference and reception issues, we generally recommend them as something to try only after exhausting the alternatives. But Kensington's descriptively named Digital FM Transmitter/Auto Charger for iPod (DFT) stands out as a rare gem in this category. You connect your iPod to the DFT via a single dock connector cable, which sends power to the iPod while grabbing the dock connector's higher-quality audio signal. You then choose the FM "broadcast" frequency via up/down tuning buttons. (You also get three handy presets, which are useful if you have to switch between stations over the course of your commute.) Audio quality and signal strength are significantly better than that of the other FM transmitters we've tested, and we like the DFT's compact size. For dockable iPods, FM transmitters don't get much better than this.

TransPod shuffle $60

Digital Lifestyle Outfitters | www.dlodirect.com

If you've got an iPod shuffle, you've probably noticed that most of the "iPod" FM transmitters and car mounts don't work with *your* iPod. DLO comes to the rescue with the TransPod shuffle: an FM transmitter, car charger, and vehicle mount all rolled into one attractive—and impressively compact—package. The TransPod plugs into your car's accessory jack and provides a sturdy base for your shuffle. Although the FM transmitter doesn't provide quite as clear a signal as that of the Kensington model also recommended here, the TransPod shuffle has four presets and is easy to tune— not something we can say about all transmitters. The TransPod also includes an audio output jack, for a direct connection to your car stereo, and an audio input jack, which lets you connect a second- ary audio source (laptop, portable DVD player, full-size iPod) and then broadcast *its* audio as well. The TransPod shuffle is currently our favorite car accessory for the iPod shuffle.

Auto Kit for iPod $40

Belkin | www.belkin.com

Car Chargers

However you decide to connect your iPod to your car stereo, you're going to want to provide the player with power—it's no fun having a dead iPod on a long road trip. If your audio hookup doesn't already supply the juice, Belkin's Auto Kit for iPod and Griffin's PowerJolt and PowerPod all do the job nicely. The Griffin accessories each feature a car-accessory-jack plug with either a USB (PowerJolt) or FireWire (PowerPod) jack at the other end. You connect your iPod via (for dockable iPods) the included dock connector cable or (for 1G and 2G iPods) a standard FireWire cable; you can plug an iPod shuffle directly into the PowerJolt's USB port. Belkin's Auto Kit—available in white or black—works only with dockable

PowerJolt and PowerPod $25

Griffin Technology | www.griffintechnology.com

PowerJolt

PowerPod

iPods, thanks to its built-in dock connector cable; however, its advantage is that it also grabs the audio signal from the iPod's dock port. It then makes that audio signal available via a built-in audio output jack with adjustable volume level—you can connect a cassette adapter or other audio cable directly to the Auto Kit.

General Accessories

In the previous chapters, we've covered iPod cases, speakers, headphones, and auto add-ons. Everything else—and there's a lot—falls under the broad category of General Accessories. From cables to camera connectors, hubs to headphone splitters, radios to remotes to recorders, this is where you'll find our favorite "other" products.

Apple iPod Camera Connector $29

Apple | http://store.apple.com

Full-size, photo-capable iPods let you transfer your pictures directly from your digital camera to your iPod for on-the-go storage, but you need an adapter to make the connection. Our favorite is Apple's own iPod Camera Connector, which plugs into your iPod's dock connector slot and provides a standard USB port; you then plug your camera's USB cable into the Camera Connector to initiate the transfer. (A good number of cameras are supported.) You'll even be able to view most images on your iPod immediately. Transfer speeds are slow, and the process sucks your iPod's battery power like mad, but the Camera Connector turns your iPod into a handy way to back up or store photos during a long vacation or a busy day of shooting.

Apple iPod Docks

Standard models, $29; color display & Universal models, $39

Apple | http://store.apple.com

It used to be that every iPod included one of Apple's handy Docks; nowadays you've got to buy it separately. Why would you want one? For starters, you can keep Apple's dock connector cable plugged into the Dock; when you want to charge or sync your iPod, you just drop it in the Dock, where the iPod sits safely upright instead of sliding around your desk. The Dock also provides a true line-level audio output jack—a better way to hook up your iPod to your home stereo than by using its headphone jack. For more functionality, check out the "color display" and Universal Docks. If you've got an iPod capable of presenting your photos or video on a television—an iPod photo, "iPod with color display," or "iPod with video"—Apple's "color display Dock" adds an S-video output for connecting your iPod to your TV. The Universal Dock includes the same video output, but adds a remote control receiver that lets you use Apple's wireless Remote to control your iPod; thanks to handy Dock inserts, the Universal Dock works with all dockable iPods. Each model-specific Dock fits its respective iPod; Universal Dock fits all dockable iPods.

Apple USB or FireWire Power Adapter $29

Apple | http://store.apple.com

Each model-specific Dock fits its respective iPod; Universal Dock fits all dockable iPods. Your iPod is charged whenever it's connected to your computer, but for those times when you don't have your computer with you—or to simply give yourself more charging options and locations—Apple's iPod Power Adapters come in handy. If you've got a full-size or mini iPod, you should get the adapter that matches your iPod's dock connector cable—USB or FireWire. If you've got an iPod shuffle or nano, the USB version is what you want. (The iPod shuffle can plug directly into the adapter's USB port.)

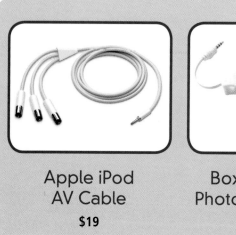

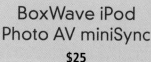

Apple iPod AV Cable	BoxWave iPod Photo AV miniSync
$19	**$25**
Apple http://store.apple.com	BoxWave www.boxwave.com

If you've got an iPod capable of presenting your photos or videos on a television—an iPod photo, "iPod with color display," or "iPod with video"—you need an AV cable or dock in order to do so. Docks are great for home use, but for showing media on the go, you want a travel-friendly cable. Apple's $19 iPod AV Cable is impressively built, with thick cables and sturdy RCA connectors. BoxWave's miniSync feels a bit flimsier but automatically retracts into a small, wind-up reel for more compact packing. Either cable will plug into your photo/color/video iPod's AV (headphone) jack and provide RCA left and right audio plugs as well as an RCA composite video plug for connecting to your television or projector. (You can also use the audio plugs on their own for connecting your iPod to a stereo for audio-only playback.)

TruePower
$30–$40

FastMac
www.fastmac.com

NuPower
$15–$35

Newer Technology/OWC
www.macsales.com

FastMac TruePower

Newer Technology NuPower

Batteries—Replacement

If you've got an older iPod with a battery that's seen better days, or even a newer iPod that's simply been overworked, one of the best "accessories" you can buy is a new battery. FastMac and Newer Technology sell a range of batteries for everything from the very first iPods to the latest photo-capable versions; Newer Tech even has one for the iPod mini. Installation of the new battery isn't trivial, but both companies provide clear instructions and the necessary tools for those brave enough to take the DIY route. If you'd rather leave such work to the professionals, both companies will perform the replacement for you for an additional $40. The best news? No matter which iPod you have, these replacement batteries will provide longer playback time than your iPod's original battery.

iPod shuffle External Battery Pack
$29

Apple
http://store.apple.com

TuneJuice
$20

Griffin Technology
www.griffintechnology.com

iPod shuffle External Battery Pack

TuneJuice

Batteries—External

If your current battery is worn out, you need a replacement; but if you simply need longer battery life than your iPod can provide, you need an extra—one that plugs into your iPod and gives it supercharged playing time. iPod shuffle owners will want to check out Apple's External Battery Pack; it adds approximately 8 hours of juice via two AAA batteries, for a total of 20 hours of playback. Griffin's TuneJuice, the smallest battery available for dockable iPods, is perfect for extending your listening time just enough to

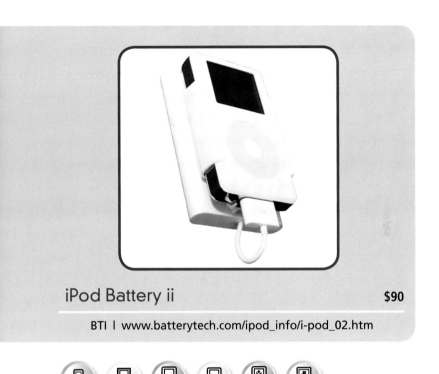

iPod Battery ii $90

BTI | www.batterytech.com/ipod_info/i-pod_02.htm

iPod Battery ii

get through the rest of the day; a single 9V battery provides 4 hours of playback time for a dead iPod or 8 additional hours to an iPod that's still running on its own. Finally, for longer battery life than you thought possible, look to BTI's Battery ii. This battery on steroids provides over 40 hours of additional playback time to dockable iPods via its own rechargeable lithium ion battery. (In fact, we often got many more than 40 hours.) The Battery ii is fairly bulky and heavy, and it's significantly more expensive than some of the other options on the market, but if we were going to be away from civilization for a week, this is the battery we'd take to keep our tunes playing.

Charger $40

Incase | www.goincase.com

If you're thinking of buying both an AC adapter *and* a car charger
for your iPod, you'll want to first take a look at Incase's generically
named Charger. At first glance, the Charger looks like an oddly
shaped iPod car adapter, and it is—it plugs into a car accessory
("cigarette lighter") outlet and provides power to any dockable
iPod via a 5-foot dock connector cable. But the side of the Charger
reveals a flip-out plug that lets you plug the unit into any U.S.-style
AC wall outlet, automatically adapting to whatever voltage is used
in your current location. The Charger also features a line-level audio
output for connecting your iPod to your car or home stereo or to
portable speakers. In other words, you get car and AC chargers in a
single unit, which saves space in your road trip bag—and money.

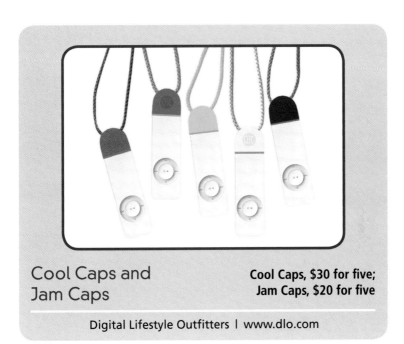

Cool Caps and Jam Caps

**Cool Caps, $30 for five;
Jam Caps, $20 for five**

Digital Lifestyle Outfitters | www.dlo.com

It's a pretty good bet that if you've got an iPod shuffle, either you or someone you know has lost their shuffle's USB cap or lanyard. Apple sells a set of three replacement caps and a lanyard for $19, but for a bit of flair and variety, check out DLO's Cool Caps and Jam Caps. Cool Caps, replacements for Apple's white lanyard attachment, come in a pack of five mix-and-match color combinations for $30. (Unlike with Apple's lanyard, you can adjust the length of each Cool Cap's rope.) Jam Caps, soft silicone replacements for Apple's white USB cap, come in a package of five colors for $20. (Even if you don't *need* a replacement cap, Jam Caps are great for keeping track of whose shuffle is whose in a multi-iPod house.) Don't need five of each? Split a pack with a friend.

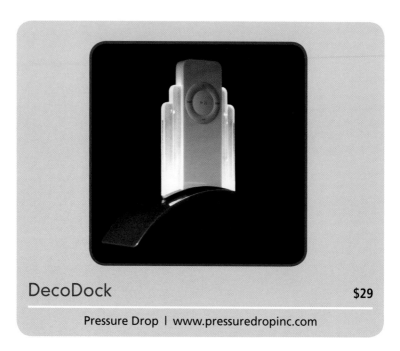

DecoDock   **$29**

Pressure Drop | www.pressuredropinc.com

Although docks for the iPod shuffle don't include a line-level audio out jack like the larger docks, they're still useful accessories: It's nice not to have to reach behind your computer to plug in and unplug your shuffle, and some computers can't accommodate the fatter-than-a-USB-plug shuffle via their own ports. But Apple's iPod shuffle Dock, which is basically a fancy USB extension cable, is pricey at $29. For the same money, you can get Pressure Drop's stylish DecoDock. It's no more functional than Apple's version, but its Art Deco–inspired design—complete with tiered translucent sides that light up—is a lot more fun to look at. The DecoDock even provides a small nub on the back to hold your shuffle's USB cap while it's docked. Like Apple's shuffle Dock, the DecoDock is pricey for what it does. But the DecoDock has something Apple's Dock doesn't: style.

General Accessories

iTrip with LCD

**Remote-jack version, \$40;
dock-connector version, \$50**

Griffin Technology | www.griffintechnology.com

Remote-jack version

Dock-connector version

FM Transmitters

Although they don't sound as good as a direct connection to your
stereo, FM transmitters—which broadcast your iPod's audio to an
open frequency that can be received by any FM radio—are popular
for their convenience and portability. I recommend several car-only
transmitters in the "Auto Accessories" chapter, but if you want to
be able to use your transmitter at home or in the office, you need

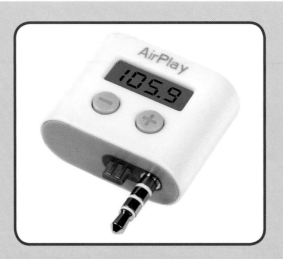

AirPlay/AirPlay2

AirPlay, $40; AirPlay2, $60

XtremeMac I www.xtrememac.com

AirPlay compatibility

AirPlay2 compatibility

one that's self-contained. Griffin's iTrip with LCD doesn't have the best range in stereo mode, but it's small enough to fit comfortably on the top or bottom of a compatible iPod; it includes an LCD screen and easy-to-use knob for choosing a broadcast frequency; and it automatically adjusts your iPod's volume to prevent distortion. And if you're having trouble getting a clear signal, a DX (mono) mode offers better range with less static. (The iTrip is available in two versions: one that connects to recent iPods with a headphone/remote jack and another that connects to the dock

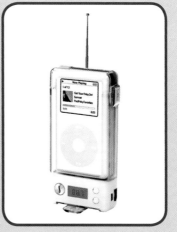

PodFreq

$99

Sonnet | www.podfreq.com

connector port of dockable iPods.) XtremeMac's AirPlay has stereo range and sound quality similar to the iTrip with LCD—although no mono mode—and is a better fit for iPod minis, thanks to its smaller size. (The AirPlay works with recent iPods with a remote/headphone jack; the AirPlay2 connects to the dock connector port of dockable iPods.) Sonnet's PodFreq, which looks and fits like a large plastic iPod case and is significantly more expensive, stands out in one other way, as well: It offers the best range and sound quality of any portable transmitter we've tested. Full-size versions of the PodFreq, which fit full-size dockable iPods, are available in white and black; a third model, in white, is made specifically for iPod minis.

Headphone Splitter   **$15**

BTI | www.batterytech.com

Sometimes you want to share your music with someone else. Problem is, your iPod's got only one headphone jack. BTI's Headphone Splitter plugs into that jack and converts it into two, so both you and your friend can listen at the same time. But what makes BTI's splitter unique is that each of the two jacks has its own rotary volume control—each listener can choose his or her own level—thus providing a solution to the eternal dilemma of headphone splitters: Which person gets to set the volume?

HomeDock   **$100**

Digital Lifestyle Outfitters | www.dlo.com

Want to hook up your iPod to your home entertainment system? You could buy one of Apple's Docks, an AC adapter, a remote control, and various cables, which might cost you well over $100. Or you could get DLO's HomeDock, which combines all this functionality into a single package. The adjustable dock fits any dockable iPod—even if the iPod is in a case. Once docked, the HomeDock charges your iPod while connecting it to your home stereo for audio and, in the case of photo- and video-capable iPods, to your TV for photo slide shows and video playback. (Audio and composite video cables are included.) The HomeDock's 14-function infrared remote control is one of the most capable on the market, even letting you navigate between playlists. Finally, the HomeDock's USB port lets you connect your iPod to your computer to sync with iTunes. Clad in black and silver, the HomeDock also looks good next to most AV equipment.

iAirPlay Charger for iPod $30

Monster Cable Products | www.monstercable.com

Spend a lot of time on planes and in cars? If so, Monster's iAirPlay is a must-have travel accessory for keeping your iPod juiced. The iAirPlay, which connects to the dock port on dockable iPods via a 1-meter cable, provides two options for charging and powering your player: an "airline power" plug that fits in the special power jacks on many newer airplanes, and an accessory jack ("cigarette lighter") adapter that fits over the airline plug for use in cars and some older airplanes that have automobile-style power jacks. Both the dock connector and airline power plugs lock in place, requiring you to release spring-loaded clips to unplug them, so you can be sure you're running off power rather than your iPod's battery.

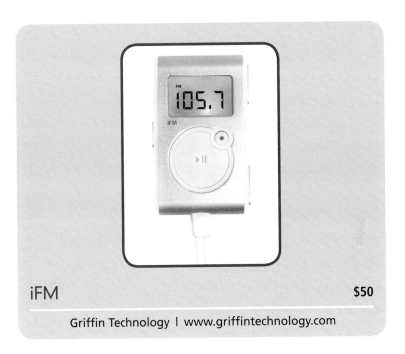

iFM $50

Griffin Technology | www.griffintechnology.com

Remote-jack version

Dock-connector version

FM radio? Wired remote? Radio and voice recorder? Griffin's modestly named iFM is all of the above in a tiny package not much bigger than Apple's own iPod remote. The FM tuner's backlit LCD display is easy to use, and six presets add to its convenience. The wired remote provides play/pause, volume, track skip/scan, and power controls. Finally, the iFM takes advantage of the voice-recording feature of full-size iPods to let you record—in low-res, mono quality—either the radio or audio picked up by the iFM's built-in microphone. (That said, if you plan on doing a lot of voice recording, you'll want Griffin's iTalk instead.) The entire iFM is only 2.1 by 1.3 by .4 inches; your headphones can plug into the iFM's own headphone jack. (The remote and FM radio features of the iFM also work with iPod minis; however, the recording function does not.)

International AC Power Adapter $30

BTI | www.batterytech.com

If you're a globetrotter, BTI's International AC Power Adapter provides compatibility with the AC outlets found in many countries around the world. At just over 2 by 2 by 1 inch, the adapter is easily packable, and a jack on the side accommodates one of the three included plugs—U.S., UK, or EU. A 6-foot cable ends in an iPod dock connector that plugs into your iPod to power and charge it.

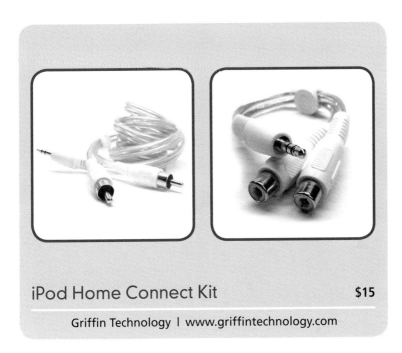

iPod Home Connect Kit $15

Griffin Technology I www.griffintechnology.com

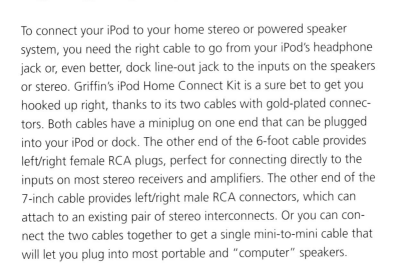

To connect your iPod to your home stereo or powered speaker system, you need the right cable to go from your iPod's headphone jack or, even better, dock line-out jack to the inputs on the speakers or stereo. Griffin's iPod Home Connect Kit is a sure bet to get you hooked up right, thanks to its two cables with gold-plated connectors. Both cables have a miniplug on one end that can be plugged into your iPod or dock. The other end of the 6-foot cable provides left/right female RCA plugs, perfect for connecting directly to the inputs on most stereo receivers and amplifiers. The other end of the 7-inch cable provides left/right male RCA connectors, which can attach to an existing pair of stereo interconnects. Or you can connect the two cables together to get a single mini-to-mini cable that will let you plug into most portable and "computer" speakers.

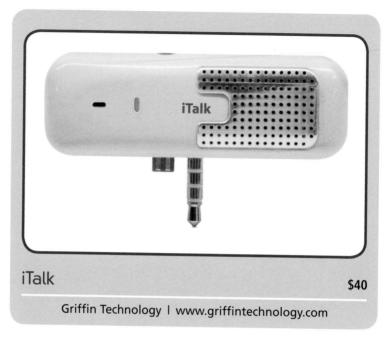

iTalk   **$40**

Griffin Technology | www.griffintechnology.com

One of the least-used features of full-size, dockable iPods is the ability to record audio; you can even download those recordings to your computer. The only caveat is that you need the right hardware. Griffin's iTalk is a compact microphone that sits on the top edge of your iPod and lets you take advantage of this functionality. Apple has limited the recording ability of most iPods to 8-bit mono, so you can't exactly record your band's next demo; but for spoken word at close range, an iTalk turns your iPod into a quality voice recorder. And for longer-range recordings, the iTalk's headphone jack doubles as a mic input, allowing you to use a higher-quality or wireless microphone. The iTalk's automatic gain control helps ensure that you're actually recording what you mean to, and you can listen to your recordings (or your iPod's music or audiobooks, for that matter) via the iTalk's built-in mono speaker or your headphones. Best of all, the iTalk's diminutive size means you won't mind bringing it along anytime you'd normally have your iPod with you. (Note that the new video-capable iPod supports 16-bit stereo recording; however, at the time of this writing, an iTalk compatible with this iPod model hadn't been announced.)

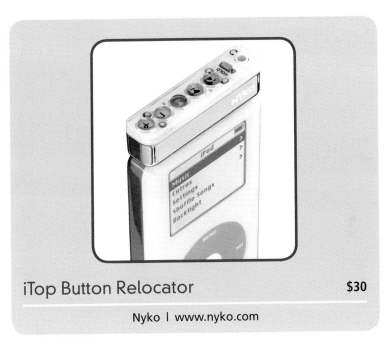

iTop Button Relocator $30

Nyko | www.nyko.com

iPods are thin enough to fit most anywhere—a pocket, a purse, you name it. The only problem is that when your iPod is in such a snug spot, you can't control it; you've got to slide it out to get to its front controls. Nyko's iTop solves this dilemma by plugging into your iPod's headphone/remote jack and giving you play/pause, track skip/scan, and volume up/down buttons right along the top edge. As long as you can see the top of your iPod, you can control it. A nice touch, so to speak, is that the iTop's buttons each have a different tactile surface, so after some practice you can "feel" your way around the buttons. (The iTop fits full-size iPods perfectly; although it works with iPod mini models, it fits awkwardly due to the mini's off-center headphone/remote jack.)

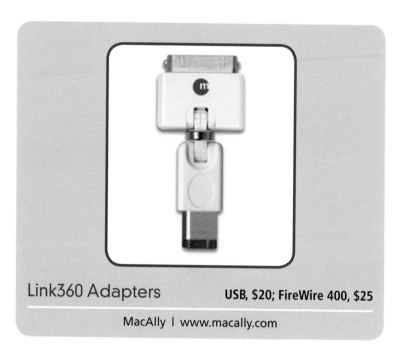

Link360 Adapters

USB, $20; FireWire 400, $25

MacAlly | www.macally.com

If you travel with your iPod and your laptop, you probably also bring along your iPod's dock cable to connect the two. MacAlly's Link360 dock adapters let you save some space in your travel bag by replacing that cable with a much more compact adapter: Each Link360 features an iPod dock connector at one end and (depending on the adapter model) a USB or FireWire plug at the other. In between the plug and dock connector is a rotating and articulating joint that allows you to connect your iPod to your computer at virtually any angle, or even offset by half an inch. And for those times when you need to use the adapter with your home computer, or with an out-of-reach port, each adapter includes a 4-foot extension cable. (A FireWire 800 version is also available, but it doesn't include the extension cable and offers no performance advantage over FireWire 400.)

General Accessories

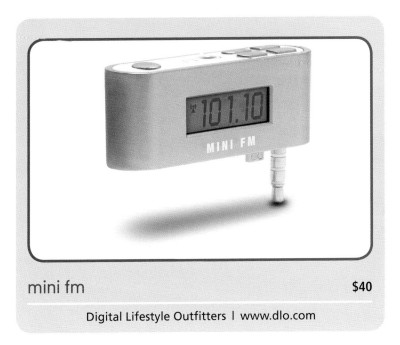

mini fm $40

Digital Lifestyle Outfitters | www.dlo.com

Wish your iPod had an FM radio? If you've got an iPod mini, you're in luck. DLO's mini fm fits perfectly on top of your iPod mini and provides an FM tuner with a backlit digital display and both manual and "scan" tuning. You switch between iPod and radio mode using the mini fm's power button; although the mini fm gets power from your iPod, it works even when your iPod is in sleep mode. And switching to the mini fm automatically pauses your iPod. The mini fm's headphone jack amplifies output 25 percent over your iPod's own jack—useful when two people are listening (such as via BTI's Headphone Splitter).

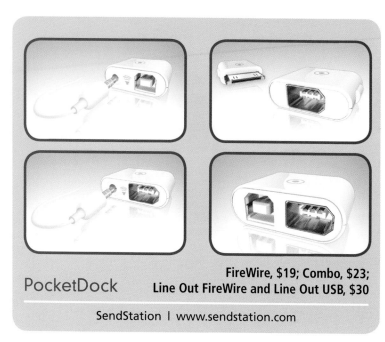

PocketDock

**FireWire, $19; Combo, $23;
Line Out FireWire and Line Out USB, $30**

SendStation I www.sendstation.com

SendStation's PocketDocks are at the top of our list of "always-
keep-these-handy" accessories for dockable iPods. Each tiny
PocketDock plugs into an iPod's dock connector port and provides
either a standard FireWire port (FireWire model); FireWire and USB
ports (Combo); a FireWire port and an audio line-out jack (Line Out
FireWire); or a line-out jack and a USB port (Line Out USB). The
FireWire and USB ports let you use any FireWire 400 or USB Type-B
cable, respectively, to charge and sync your iPod, and the line-out
jacks provide access to the dock port's higher-quality, line-level
audio output. In other words, PocketDocks are pocket versions
of Apple's iPod docks, only more flexible, since you don't need a
special cable to use them—keep a PocketDock in your bag and you
never have to worry about forgetting your dock connector cable
again. (A nice bonus: The Line Out versions even include audio
cables to connect your iPod to your stereo or speakers.)

naviPro eX
$50

TEN Technology
www.tentechnology.com

RemoteTunes
$50

Targus
www.targus.com

TEN Technology naviPro eX

Targus RemoteTunes

Remote Controls

Hook up your iPod to your stereo, and you've got your entire music library at your fingertips. Well, not quite—your stereo is probably across the room from where you're listening, so unless you've got really long arms, your iPod is out of reach. You need an iPod remote control. Some of the products recommended in this book, such as DLO's HomeDock and Kensington's Stereo Dock, have a remote control built in, but there are also a good number of remotes out there that you can buy separately. Most work similarly: A small receiver plugs into your iPod (via either its headphone/remote jack or dock connector port); a small, hand-held remote control sends signals to that receiver to control the iPod. However, the two models here stood out from the crowd in our testing.

Targus's RemoteTunes (also available as the ABT iJet) provides the standard iPod remote functions—play/pause, track skip/scan, and volume up/down—via a small, water-resistant remote that is our favorite in terms of layout and usability. The RemoteTunes has the longest range of any remote we've seen, and since it uses radio-frequency (RF) technology, the remote's signal can travel through walls. The RemoteTunes also includes a nice accessory package: a clear acrylic stand for your iPod, a mounting bracket/belt clip for the remote, and a mini-to-RCA cable for connecting your iPod to your home stereo. (Note: If you've got one of the very first iPod photo models, these iPods are incompatible with RF-based remotes; you'll want to check out the infrared-based naviPro eX instead.)

TEN Technologies' naviPro eX has more functionality than any other remote on the market, providing the standard buttons but also allowing you to switch between playlists, switch between albums, skip chapters in audiobooks, and toggle shuffle and repeat modes. (Thanks to all these buttons, the naviPro's remote is also larger and easier to hold than any other.) Unlike the Remote-Tunes, the naviPro eX uses infrared (IR) technology, which means it requires a direct line of sight between the remote and the receiver, and it has a shorter maximum range. However, one benefit of IR is that many "learning" remotes can learn the naviPro eX's commands. (And the naviPro eX is compatible with early iPod photo models, unlike RF remotes.)

Note that both of these remotes connect to the headphone/remote jack of 3G, 4G, and photo/color iPods; at the time of this writing, dock-connector versions (for compatibility with the iPod nano and video-capable iPods) had not yet been announced. If you've got a nano or video iPod, Apple's Universal Dock includes a remote receiver, but you need to buy the Remote itself separately. Both the Targus and TEN remotes also work with the iPod mini, but thanks to the mini's off-center remote/headphone jack, the remote receivers fit a bit awkwardly.

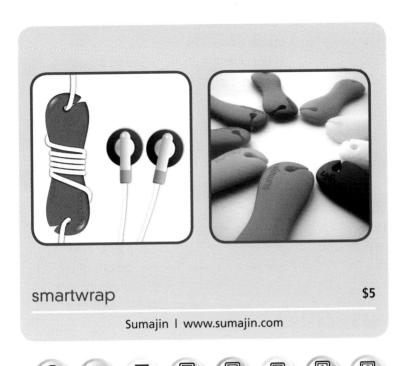

smartwrap $5

Sumajin | www.sumajin.com

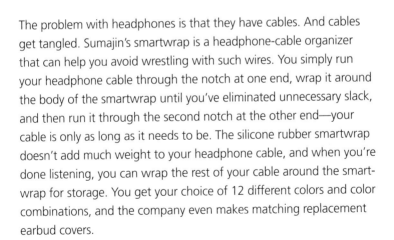

The problem with headphones is that they have cables. And cables get tangled. Sumajin's smartwrap is a headphone-cable organizer that can help you avoid wrestling with such wires. You simply run your headphone cable through the notch at one end, wrap it around the body of the smartwrap until you've eliminated unnecessary slack, and then run it through the second notch at the other end—your cable is only as long as it needs to be. The silicone rubber smartwrap doesn't add much weight to your headphone cable, and when you're done listening, you can wrap the rest of your cable around the smart-wrap for storage. You get your choice of 12 different colors and color combinations, and the company even makes matching replacement earbud covers.

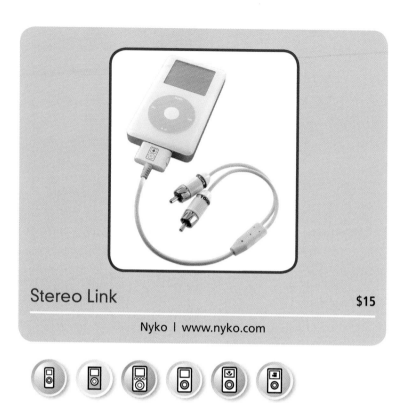

Stereo Link $15

Nyko | www.nyko.com

To hook up your dockable iPod to your home stereo, you need the right cable—one with a stereo miniplug at one end to connect to your iPod and left/right RCA plugs at the other to connect to most stereos. Ideally, you would also want to grab the higher-quality, line-level audio provided by your iPod's dock port instead of simply plugging the cable into the iPod's headphone jack. Does that mean you need to spring for one of Apple's $29–$39 Docks and then spend another $10–$20 for a decent audio cable? Not at all. Nyko's Stereo Link gives you exactly what you need via a single cable that features a dock connector at one end and quality left and right RCA plugs at the other. You lose the Dock's ability to hold your iPod upright, and when using the Stereo Link you can't charge or sync your iPod, but for $15, the Stereo Link is the least expensive option on the market—and it doesn't sacrifice sound quality to achieve that low price.

Stereo Dock for iPod $90

Kensington I www.kensington.com

We recommend DLO's HomeDock for an all-in-one way to connect a photo- or video-capable iPod to both a home entertainment system and your computer, but if you simply want to connect your iPod to your home stereo, Kensington's Stereo Dock is an attractive alternative. After plugging the Stereo Dock into an AC outlet and your stereo—adapter and cables are included—you simply plop your iPod in the Stereo Dock and press Play. (Your iPod is even charged while docked.) The Stereo Dock's infrared remote control provides only the typical iPod-remote functionality—play/pause, track skip/scan, and volume—but it's larger than most and includes backlit buttons, making it one of our favorites to use. And although list price of the Stereo Dock is $90, street prices are just more than half that, making it a no-brainer when you compare it with the combined cost of one of Apple's docks and a remote control (which still wouldn't include an AC adapter).

TuneStage for iPod $170

Belkin I www.belkin.com

When you're listening to your iPod through your home stereo, an iPod remote control is almost a must-have accessory; in fact, I recommend several models in this book. However, such remotes have two limitations: You can't see your iPod's screen from across the room, and you get only basic playback control. Belkin's TuneStage turns this scenario on its head by connecting a small transmitter to your iPod's headphone/remote jack and then sending your audio wirelessly to a receiver connected to your stereo or speaker system. Your iPod and its famously intuitive interface remain in your hand, the best "iPod remote" ever. And the TuneStage uses Bluetooth wireless technology, which means static-free performance and crystal-clear audio up to 30 feet away; you can even transmit through walls.

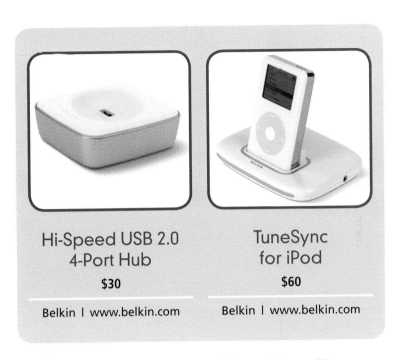

Hi-Speed USB 2.0 4-Port Hub

$30

Belkin | www.belkin.com

TuneSync for iPod

$60

Belkin | www.belkin.com

Hi-Speed USB 2.0
4-Port Hub

   TuneSync for iPod

USB Hubs

If you've got a number of USB devices in addition to your iPod, chances are your Mac is running out of USB ports—you need a hub. If you're also thinking about getting an iPod Dock, consider Belkin's dock/hub combos instead. The Hi-Speed USB 2.0 4-Port Hub provides three USB ports in back, along with a single port on top that's perfect for docking your iPod shuffle; at only a dollar more than Apple's iPod shuffle Dock, it's a relative bargain. The TuneSync for iPod provides five powered USB 2.0 ports on the back, along with a dock on the top for full-size, mini, and (in a pinch) nano iPods. And like Apple's Dock, the TuneSync includes a line-level audio output jack to connect your iPod to a stereo or speakers. Sure, it's twice as much as Apple's Dock, but then you'd still have to buy a USB 2.0 hub—and have two peripherals on your desk instead of one. Both hubs are white and gray for that signature iPod look.

Playlist Review URLs

For more information about products discussed in this book—including reviews, specifications, and for many products, shopping links to help you find the lowest price—you can visit each product's resource page on the Playlist Web site. To do so, type the product's Playlist URL, playlistmag.com/####, in your Web browser address field (where #### is the four-digit product number listed below).

A

A-1 Quality Products iKeychain, 2100
Agent 18 mini Shock cases, 2101
AKG K 14 P headphones, 2102
AKG K 26 P headphones, 2103
Altec Lansing FX6021 home speakers, 2104
Altec Lansing inMotion iM7 portable speakers, 2105
Altec Lansing inMotion iM716 headphones, 2106
Apple iPod AV Cable, 2107
Apple iPod Camera Connector, 2108
Apple iPod Docks, 2109
Apple iPod nano armband, 2110
Apple iPod shuffle armband, 2111
Apple iPod shuffle External Battery Pack, 2112
Apple iPod shuffle sport case, 2113
Apple USB or FireWire Power Adapter, 2114
AVB Cassette Adapter for iPod auto accessory, 2115

B

Bang & Olufsen A8 headphones, 2116
Belkin Auto Kit for iPod, 2117
Belkin Hi-Speed USB 2.0 4-Port Hub, 2118
Belkin TuneStage for iPod, 2119
Belkin TuneSync for iPod, 2120
Beyerdynamic DT 231 headphones, 2121
Bose SoundDock home speakers, 2122
BoxWave iPod Photo AV miniSync, 2123
BTI Headphone Splitter, 2124
BTI International AC Power Adapter, 2125
BTI iPod Battery ii, 2126

C

Cambridge SoundWorks Model Twelve portable speakers, 2127
Contour Design Showcase cases, 2128
Convertec leather cases, 2129

D

Delarew Designs Delapod bags, 2130
Denison IceLink Plus auto accessory, 2131
Digital Lifestyle Outfitters Cool Caps and Jam Caps, 2132
Digital Lifestyle Outfitters HomeDock, 2133
Digital Lifestyle Outfitters iBoom portable speakers, 2134
Digital Lifestyle Outfitters mini fm, 2135
Digital Lifestyle Outfitters TransPod shuffle auto accessory, 2136

E

Etymotic Research ER-4P headphones, 2137
Etymotic Research ER-6i headphones, 2138

F

FastMac TruePower batteries, 2139
Focal-JMlab iCub home speakers, 2140
Future SonicsXtremeMac FS1 canalphones, 2141

G

Grado SR 60 headphones, 2142
Griffin Technology iFM, 2143

Griffin Technology iPod Home Connect Kit, 2144
Griffin Technology iSqueez iPod stands, 2145
Griffin Technology iTalk microphones, 2146
Griffin Technology iTrip with LCD, 2147
Griffin Technology PowerJolt and PowerPod auto accessories, 2148
Griffin Technology SmartDeck auto accessory, 2149
Griffin Technology TuneJuice, 2150

H

Harman Kardon Drive+Play auto accessory, 2151
Harman Kardon Soundsticks II home speakers, 2152
HeadRoom AirHead/BitHead headphone amp, 2153
HeadRoom Complete HeadCase headphone bags, 2154

I

iHome Audio iH5 clock radio home speakers, 2155
iMojo shuffle Sweats cases, 2156
Incase Charger, 2157
Incase Folio for iPod U2 special edition cases, 2158
iSkins cases, 2159

J

JBL Creature II home speakers, 2160
JBL On Tour portable speakers, 2161
JBL On Stage II home speakers, 2162

K

Kate Spade Broome Street leather cases, 2163
Kensington Digital FM Transmitter/Auto Charger for iPod, 2164
Kensington Stereo Dock for iPod, 2165
Klipsch iFi home speakers, 2166
Klipsch ProMedia Ultra 2.0 home speakers, 2167
Koss KSC-75 headphones, 2168
Koyono BlackCoat T cases, 2169

L

Logic 3 i-Station portable speakers, 2170
Logic 3 i-Station shuffle portable speakers, 2171
Logitech mm50 portable speakers, 2172
Logitech Wireless Headphones for iPod, 2173
Logitech Z-4i home speakers, 2174

M

MacAlly Link360 adapters, 2175
MacAlly PodWave portable speakers, 2176
Marware SportGrip for iPod shuffle cases, 2177
Marware SportSuit Convertible cases, 2178
Marware TrailVue cases, 2179
Matias iPod Armor cases, 2180
Miniot iWood cases, 2181
Monster Cable Products iAirPlay Charger for iPod, 2182

N

Newer Technology/OWC NuPower batteries, 2183
Nyko iTop Button Relocator, 2184
Nyko Stereo Link, 2185
Nyko Universal Car Mount auto accessory, 2186

Index